Becoming a Pioneer

Becoming a Pioneer

A Book Series

The Month-by-Month Guide
to Doubling Your Business and
Taking Over Your Industry in a Year

Bimal Shah

Book 9: Build Sustainable Replicable Systems

Becoming a Pioneer - Book 9

© Copyright 2023 by Bimal Shah

All rights reserved. No part of this publication can be reproduced, distributed, or transmitted in any form or by any means, including photocopying, recording, or other electronic or mechanical methods, without the prior written permission of the publisher, except in the case of brief quotations embodied in critical reviews and certain other noncommercial uses permitted by copyright law.

Neither the author nor the publisher assumes any responsibility or liability whatsoever on behalf of the consumer or reader of this material. Any perceived slight of any individual or organization is purely unintentional.

The resources in this book are provided for informational purposes only and neither the author nor the publisher can be held responsible for the use of the information provided within this book. Please always consult a trained professional before making any decision regarding the topics in this book.

ISBN: 979-8-8692-0653-4 Paperback

ISBN: 979-8-8692-0654-1 E-Book

Published by:

TheOneYearBreakthrough.com

For more information, email: Bimal@theoneyearbreakthrough.com

Rajparth Achievers, LLC
5550 Glades Road, Suite 500
Boca Raton, FL 33431

Connect with Pioneers around the World. Every Month. With the book purchase, you are a member. No strings attached.

Join Me and walk away with personalized insights for you in the monthly Club meeting.

Get Your Free Membership here.
https://bit.ly/ThePioneersClub

Learn Exponentially More.

This book is most effective when paired with its training program, enabling you to "Systematize" everything within your business and build replicable systems. Through this approach, you can empower your team to build recurring sustainable growth systems that can last forever. This systematic approach sets the stage for achieving exponential growth in your business within a year.

Get Your Free Video Training at:
https://bit.ly/TheSustainableReplicableSystems

To my wife, Ami, and our daughters, Rajvi, and Parthvi. This book would not have been possible without the efforts of Ami with the editing. Her strength and support are priceless. Also, I am indebted to my daughters for their invaluable insight into the structure and design. My family is everything to me.

I love them with all my heart.

Content

Author's Preface	1
Making Pioneers! —The What and Why	1
Introduction	8
Week 1 Before-During-After: The Hidden System of Every Successful Business	9 9
Week 2 Inside the Toolbox: Processes, Checklists, and Beyond	37 37
Week 3 All Your Platforms to Systematize	59 59
Week 4 The Five Dials of The Rinse and Repeat Systems	81 81
Conclusion	105
About the Author	107
Some Accolades for Bimal's Work	109

Author's Preface

Making Pioneers! —The What and Why

What is a Pioneer?

A pioneer is unique and different from the rest.

To be a pioneer, you need to be the Only One at something. This book is about breaking all the barriers and obstacles you have in your life, work, habits, and mindset. The purpose of this book is to bring a 10x to a 100x transformation in your perspective about yourself—to assist you in realizing your true potential in a very short time.

Why be a Pioneer?

God has made every human being unique and different. When every human becomes unique and different, the whole world can work in harmony. Becoming a pioneer happens through stages and discoveries. I wrote this book with the intent of creating the essential stages and discoveries you will need at each step. Drawing from my own experiences, it builds fresh perspectives that can take your business to the next level.

Editor Ami Shah with Author Bimal Shah

How to Get the Most Out of This Book Series

Go slow. This is a book you do not want to read fast. Write in the margins. Scribble in it, make notes and use sticky notes. Carry this book with you wherever you go. This is your book and customized manual to help you at least double what you believe you can do in a year.

Even if you answer one question from this book, it will have a positive impact on your life or business. Below are five ways you can make the most out of it:

1. Read first, think second, and then write: Read a sentence or two or a paragraph. Think about it and answer the questions that follow.

2. Go digging: Look up something in your business or your personal life related to the question. And then come back and answer the question.

3. Use Sharp Pencils with an eraser on top: Instead of using pens, please use pencils, as while you are writing your thoughts on the questions, the answers will change in due course.

4. Watch the video before you start reading: In the video, you will get a lot more insights into the book itself. It will walk you through powerful elements to scale.

5. Scan the QR CODE and save the QR CODE link in your Notes on your Smartphone: When you answer a specific question, look up the links listed in the Link Tree. See if there is a resource for the challenge you are trying to overcome. The Link Tree is very useful. It works like magic; you will find new and amazing things each time you look.

Special Advice for Using This Book
in Uncertain Economic Times

As we all know, the future is questionable. I recommend using this book series in a sequential order to stabilize and speed up your income growth. Follow the advice in the acronym UNCERTAIN:

U-Unique - Discover from each book how to become unique. Book #5 lists elements to leverage to be unique.

N- New – Apply the different tools and systems taught in Book #1, book #9, and Book #11. To bring in the new you in record time.

C-Confidence – Use the Confidence Journey tool from book #5. To build daily confidence in your journey.

E-Empathy – Use the Self-Empathy skills from book #10 and book #2 (this one). To deal with uncertainties, biggest pains, or frustrations.

R-Resilience – Lay the foundation for building resilience with a powerful vision in book #1. Apply Book #12 resiliency skills.

T-Transparency – Discover from book #3, book #4, and book #6 how to use good or bad transparency. This is to propel you and your business to the next level.

A-Audacious – From book #1, book #13, and book #6 you will discover how to maintain and chase audacious goals.

I-Implementation – From Book #7 on Sprints and Book #8 on Leadership. Throughout each book in the series, you will become a master implementor.

N-Next Steps – Every single chapter in each book helps you build your customized next steps. There is no way you can't stabilize or grow if you follow all the steps you built by yourself, using this book series.

Becoming a
PIONEER

Special Advice for Using this Book Series in Prosperous Economic Times

When times are good, you can make them better by using this book series with the acronym AWESOME as follows:

A-Algorithms - In business when there are a lot of opportunities coming your way, you need to apply an algorithm: a one-line business plan. Build your customized scale from algorithms listed in book #4 and book #13.

W-Wins – At the end of every chapter, you celebrate your wins. In book #5 you have the tools that make it a recurring habit.

E-Extra –There is no traffic beside you in the extra mile. In book #12, you will have the systems to drive on no-traffic roads.

S-Surprisers –What to do when your team and customers surprise you. You are bound to get surprised quite often. Discover the best responses in book #1, book #2 (this book), book #3, book #4, and book #10.

O-Omnipresence –Through book #6 and book #3, you will build your systems. Through book #11 you will build your own skill sets. Through book #9 you will build the platforms. In book #10 you will have the systems and tools to automate omnipresence.

M-Multiplication –When times are good, you need systems to multiply. Through Book #1 you will lay the foundation for multiplication. Through Book #7 you will build the skills. Through Book #8 and Book #9, you will build the traits for becoming a multiplier and the systems essential for it.

E-Extinguishers –When things are happening like rapid fire, you need a different kind of extinguisher. This is to extinguish the fires and keep up the pace you are moving at. Build your fire extinguishers from book #5.

Introduction

This book is written with the intent to make an immediate positive impact on you, the reader. Because of this reason, there are more questions, with immensely valuable tools, resources, stories, and action steps.

This way you can even answer one question and see a positive impact. I want you to have notes all over this book and that's why there are a lot of spaces for you to make this book your "own unique book."

There are many self-development and business books out there. I wrote this series to direct your thinking in a specific way. So, sit back and relax while you read.

There is one topic in this book that allows you to go deep. It also makes a real positive difference in the least amount of time. Even if you spend five minutes reading this book, you will feel the transformation.

What's unique and different about this book is that this is the book series you will cherish forever. It has your goals, your plans, your actions, and most of all a system you can use every year.

The system consists of a series of 13 stages. Each last 4 weeks; you can achieve your 3-year goal in One Year. Besides, I didn't want to write about anything you already knew.

Alongside the questions for you to answer are tools to use. And some practical solutions you can put in place and see great results.

I hope this book will make a more positive impact on your life. For your convenience, I have left you enough space to answer each question. I have noticed many people have bigger handwriting and need more space to write!

Eagerly look forward to meeting you in Part X!

Week 1

Before-During-After: The Hidden System of Every Successful Business

I used to believe that everything followed a linear path from beginning to end. However, I've come to understand that there's a precursor to the beginning itself. This realization led me to develop the before-during-after system, which serves as a framework to organize all aspects systematically. Allow me to illustrate this with an example.

Before	During	After
(e.g., Knowing Who You Want to Hire)	(e.g., Attracting the Right Candidates)	(e.g. Successful Hiring Process)
https://bit.ly/MyDreamEmployee		https://bit.ly/TheHiringSystemThatWorks

```
       | -------------------- | -------------------- |
         Common Ground: "Successful Candidate Hired"
```

In this representation:

"Before," "During," and "After" are labeled stages of the hiring process. Each stage contains examples of activities or processes relevant to that stage (e.g., discovering the right position, the system to attract the right candidates, and the ideal hiring process for the same).

The overlapping area represents the common ground where all three stages converge, leading to the desired outcome ("Successful Candidate Hired").

This structure illustrates how the before-during-after system applies to the hiring process, starting from first knowing exactly who you want to hire, attracting the right candidates with the right message, and culminating in the successful hiring of a new employee through the right hiring process.

When it comes to hiring, I have discovered that one of the biggest mistakes you make is to hire based on title and not go deep into exactly who you want to hire. Most of the time, the perception of who you want to hire and who you want to hire are two completely different elements. This is the first step in getting the right hires for your company. This is why I developed a FREE tool to avoid the biggest mistake in hiring and you can access it at https://bit.ly/MyDreamEmployee.

In business, every outcome has three parts: before, during, and after. This goes for starting a new product, running a marketing campaign, or managing a project. Knowing these parts well is important for doing well.

Before we start, let's imagine some things:

What does success look like for your customer?
_____
_____
_____
_____
_____

What is(are) the dream(s) outcome(s) they're hoping for?
_____
_____
_____
_____
_____

Think about the five things that need to happen to make that dream come true results for your customer.
1._____
_____
2._____
_____

WEEK 1

3._____

4._____

5._____

Then, let's zoom out and look at the overall journey.
What are the top five obstacles you might face along the way?

1._____

2._____

3._____

4._____

5._____

What can you do at the beginning to avoid those obstacles and solve most of the problems that may occur in the middle or during the journey? (Most of the time you get stuck in the middle and to end right, you must begin right).

1._____

2._____

3._____

4._____

5._____

Good job. Now let's proceed to the chapter breakdown. Let's see how each part helps you reach your goals. I'll give you an illustration on the next page and some questions, tools, exercises, and ways of thinking to help you avoid mistakes.

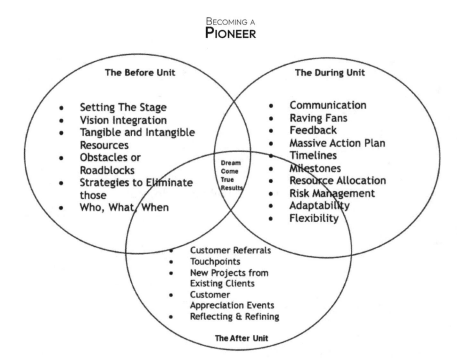

Before: Setting the Stage

Imagine you're getting ready to start something amazing—a new business, a big project, or a personal dream. Before you begin, it's really important to get things set up well, like getting everything ready before a big show. This first part, called "Setting the Stage," is where you plan carefully, think strategically, and gather what you need to make sure you do great.

First things first, you need to be clear about where you're headed—the main goal you want to reach. Whether it's starting a new product, reaching more customers, or making your business run smoother, knowing your goals is super important. It's like marking your destination on a map before you start your trip—you must know where you're going to figure out the best way to get there. Take a moment to think about these three important questions:

1. Where do you want to go?

_____
_____
_____
_____

WEEK 1

Is this destination in line with your 25-year Vision, 5-year moonshot, 3-year goal, and The One Year Breakthrough Blueprint? ❏ Y ❏ N

If yes, then that is great. If not, please go to Book #1 of the series and make sure you have the right long-term goals and that your short-term actions and decisions are in line with your long-term goals.
What are the roadblocks that you may face along the journey?

_____
_____
_____
_____
_____

2. Based on the roadblocks and the destination, What specific preparation do you need to do in the before unit to set the stage for a successful journey?

1._____
_____
2._____
_____
3._____
_____
4._____
_____
5._____
_____

What are the roadblocks stopping you from setting the stage?

_____
_____
_____
_____
_____

3. How would you eliminate those roadblocks?

_____
_____
_____
_____
_____

Who needs to do what by when to eliminate those obstacles and effectively set the stage in the before unit?

_____
_____
_____
_____
_____

Great job! Now you have set the stage for the before unit and you are ready to proceed to the next unit that is the during unit.

After you know where you want to go, it's time to plan how to get there—the strategy you'll use. This means figuring out the steps and things you need to do to move from where you are now to where you want to be. Think of it like drawing a map for your trip, showing the roads you'll take and the important places you'll see along the way.

What do you need to do after setting the stage to begin your journey to achieve your goals?

_____
_____
_____
_____
_____

Even if you have great plans, they might not work well if you don't have the right stuff. That's why the next step is gathering all the things you need to succeed. This means getting tangible things like money, tools, and materials, as well as intangible things like knowledge and skills. Think of it like gathering all the tools and materials you need to build something—you need the right stuff to make your idea come to life. You can refer to Book #4 in the series for "KASH FLOW" to understand the intangible resources you need to have or develop. Yes, it is "KASH FLOW" with a K to build real cash flow in your business.

What are examples of tangible resources needed for success, like funds, equipment, and materials?

1._____
2._____
3._____
4._____

WEEK 1

5._____

6._____

7._____

What are the intangible resources, such as knowledge, skills, and expertise, you need to achieve your goals?

1._____

2._____

3._____

4._____

5._____

6._____

7._____

How do you plan to get them (tangible and intangible things) you need?

_____

_____

_____

_____

_____

Great job! You are gradually figuring it out.

However, every journey has problems and difficulties. In this part, it's important to expect possible issues and make backup plans to deal with them. Whether it's not having enough money, facing logistical problems, or dealing with unexpected risks, being ready to handle challenges will help you stay on track toward your goals.

What are the potential roadblocks that could arise during your journey?

1._____

_____

2._____

_____

3._____

_____

4._____

_____

5._____

_____

What are your plans or strategies to curb them?

1. _____

2. _____

3. _____

4. _____

5. _____

Who needs to do what by when to eliminate those obstacles effectively?

_____
_____
_____
_____
_____

Well done! You have successfully prepared for every obstacle. You are good to go.

The "Before Unit: Setting the Stage" phase is about getting ready for success. It's about planning, strategizing, and gathering what you need before jumping into action. If you put effort into this early phase, you'll be more likely to succeed and have an easier time as you go along. So, take the time to get things set up well, and you'll see your dreams start to come true.

The During Unit: Execution in Motion

During the "Dreams Come True Results - Execution in Motion" phase, it's crucial to prioritize achieving dream-come-true results for your customers. When you achieve "dream-come-true" results for your customers, you achieve "dream-come-true" results for yourself.

Example: Amazon has three pillars where they deliver 'dream-come-true' results-options, delivery, and pricing. You can find almost anything you want to buy on Amazon. Their delivery is the fastest that is known in the industry. They provide price comparisons to their products right on each product. They have thorough product reviews, descriptions, and pictures for their best-sellers and many others. This provides dream-come-true results for shoppers and for Amazon as well.

These results represent the pinnacle of customer satisfaction and are achieved through three key elements:

1. *Consistent Communication with Your Customer or making it very easy for the customer to communicate with you*: This involves going above and beyond in communication, ensuring that you are always available, or you have made it very easy for your customer to chat or call your customer service, get an instant answer, or video answers to FAQs, and responsive to your customer's needs, even exceeding their expectations in terms of communication frequency and depth. Zappos, before selling

2. *Better Than Expected Results - Making Them Raving Fans*: Delivering results that surpass your customers' expectations is essential for turning them into loyal raving fans of your brand. When you consistently deliver outcomes that go above and beyond what they anticipated, you create a strong emotional connection and solidify customer loyalty. There are three levels of customer service- Sacrifice, Satisfaction, and Surprise.

1. *Sacrifice*: Have you ever experienced that you got less than what you paid for or what was communicated? Would you ever buy from them again if they aren't willing to do anything for their mistake? Exactly.

2. *Satisfaction*: Satisfaction is the level of customer service where you just got what you expected. You aren't necessarily very happy, and you aren't sad either. Would you buy the same product or service if you get the same experience or product for less? Exactly.

3. *Surprise*: Surprise is where you deliver better-than-expected results. Have you bought or experienced something where you got a lot more than what was expected, and the team went above and beyond to deliver great outcomes to you? Would you have any reason to buy that product or service from someone else? Exactly.

Delivering surprises and better-than-expected results, going above and beyond makes raving fans and the word spreads faster than you can ever imagine.

3. *Feedback for Improvement*: Actively seeking feedback from your customers and using it to improve your products or services is critical for ongoing success. Solicit for feedback and incorporate it into your

BECOMING A
PIONEER

processes. Surveys are very useful and ask for them at every opportunity. Whether the customer fills it out or how many fill out is irrelevant- you doing it consistently is relevant. When you ask for feedback, make it very authentic and not a solicitation. A true feedback seeker will get the feedback from the customer. It demonstrates your commitment to continuous improvement and customer satisfaction.

How can you ensure consistent communication with your customers, exceeding their expectations and fostering strong relationships?

_____

_____

_____

_____

_____

What strategies can you implement to consistently deliver better-than-expected results, turning your customers into loyal fans of your brand?

_____

_____

_____

_____

_____

How will you actively seek feedback from your customers and use it to improve your products or services, demonstrating your commitment to their satisfaction and success?

_____

_____

_____

_____

_____

Now that you have gathered all the necessary resources for your journey and prepared for the obstacles ahead, it is time to execute. Let's put your plans into action.

Putting Plans into Action: This is when ideas become real. It's where you start doing things. After planning carefully, it's time to get to work. This phase is when you move from thinking about things to doing them. It's about taking real steps towards your goals, using the energy you built up during the planning stage.

WEEK 1

Are you ready to transition from planning to action? ❏ Y ❏ N

What steps will you take to initiate implementation effectively?

1._____

2._____

3._____

4._____

5._____

How do you plan to maintain the continuity between the planning phase and the execution phase to ensure a seamless transition?

Execution Timeline and Milestones: Let's talk about how important it is to set a clear timeline and smaller goals for what you're doing. It's about taking your big goals and making them into smaller, doable tasks, and then giving yourself deadlines to finish them.

During the "Execution Timelines and Milestones" unit, let's consider an example here, such as launching a new marketing campaign. The project could include various stages and milestones[9], such as:

1. Planning Phase:
    - Define campaign objectives and target audience.
    - Conduct market research and competitor analysis.
    - Develop a marketing strategy and messaging framework.

Timeline: 0-2 weeks

Milestone: Completion of the campaign objectives and target audience identification.

2. Execution Phase:

- Create marketing materials, including ads, social media posts, and email campaigns.
- Set up tracking mechanisms to monitor campaign performance.
- Launch the campaign across selected channels, such as social media platforms, email newsletters, and advertising networks.

Timeline: 4 – 6 weeks

Milestone: Successful creation and deployment of marketing materials.

3. Monitoring and Optimization:

- Monitor campaign performance in real time, analyzing key metrics like click-through rates, conversion rates, and ROI.
- Adjust the campaign strategy based on performance data, such as tweaking ad copy or targeting criteria.
- Continuously optimize the campaign to maximize effectiveness and achieve desired outcomes.

Timeline: ongoing

Milestone: Continuous monitoring and optimization of the campaign based on performance metrics.

These milestones and timelines help break down the larger goal of writing a book into smaller, achievable tasks with deadlines to track progress.

This way, you make a plan that helps you know what to do and when and gives you a way to see how well you're doing and stay responsible as you go along.

Have you established a timeline for your implementation process?
❑ Y ❑ N

What are your milestones for the execution?
1._____
_____
2._____
_____

WEEK 1

3. _____

4. _____

5. _____

Can you provide examples of specific milestones you will set to track progress and ensure that your implementation stays on track?

1. _____

2. _____

3. _____

4. _____

5. _____

Great work! Don't forget to celebrate yourself when you reach a milestone. Here are easier ways to celebrate your achievements:

1. Reward Yourself: Treat yourself to something special, like a nice meal, a relaxing day, or buying something you like.
2. Reflect and Be Proud: Think about what you've achieved and be proud of yourself. Write it down or tell someone about it.
3. Celebrate with Friends or Family: Share your success with loved ones. You could have a small party or just spend time together.
4. Take Pictures or Write About It: Capture the moment with photos or write about your experience so you can remember it later.
5. Plan Something Fun: Plan a fun activity for yourself, like going for a hike, watching a movie, or doing something you enjoy.
6. Set New Goals: Think about what you want to do next and set new goals for yourself.
7. Relax and Take Time for Yourself: Take a break and do something relaxing or enjoyable, like reading a book or going for a walk.
8. Be Kind to Yourself: Take care of yourself by doing things that make you happy and feel good.

BECOMING A
PIONEER

Celebrating your achievements is important, so make sure to do something special for yourself when you reach a milestone.

How do you plan to celebrate and recognize your milestones to keep yourself feeling good about your progress?

Allocation of Resources: We'll make sure we have the right people, money, and materials to do what we need to do. Having enough of these things is important for getting things done and reaching our goals. We'll use our resources wisely, so we don't waste anything. To do this, we'll assign tasks to people based on what they're good at, so everyone can help effectively. We'll also be careful with our money, spending it on things that will help us the most. And we'll try not to waste materials by recycling and using them wisely. This act will help us get more done and reach our goals faster.

Do you have the necessary resources, including people, money, and materials, to achieve your plans effectively? ❏ Y ❏ N

If yes, how will you allocate them to ensure the efficient utilization of resources while minimizing waste to maximize productivity?

How will you ensure that financial resources are allocated in a manner that aligns with your objectives and priorities?

WEEK 1

Managing Risks and Uncertainties: In this part, we'll talk about dealing with risks and uncertainties that might cause problems when we're doing things. It's about thinking ahead and coming up with ways to deal with things that could go wrong, so our project keeps going smoothly. Handling risks before they happen can stop things from going wrong and keep us moving forward, even if things are uncertain.

To manage risks and uncertainties:

1. Identify Potential Risks: Think about what could go wrong and make a list of possible problems or uncertainties that might come up during the project.

2. Analyze Risks: Figure out how likely each risk is to happen and how much of an impact it could have on the project if it does.

3. Develop Strategies: Come up with plans to deal with each risk. This might involve finding ways to prevent the risk from happening or having a plan ready to fix things if it does.

4. Implement Risk Management Plans: Put your strategies into action and make sure everyone involved knows what to do if a risk occurs.

5. Monitor and Adjust: Keep an eye on things as the project progresses and be ready to adjust your plans if new risks arise or if the situation changes.

Be proactive in addressing risks before they become problems. It will keep your project on track and ensure its success, even in uncertain circumstances.

What are the potential risks and uncertainties that may arise during the implementation phase?

_____

_____

_____

_____

_____

BECOMING A
PIONEER

How do you plan to address them?

_____
_____
_____
_____
_____

Adaptability and Flexibility: During the project, being adaptable and flexible is super important for success. It means being ready to change your plans if things don't go as expected. Let's imagine a business scenario to understand this better.

Imagine you're starting a new business selling handmade crafts. You have a plan to sell them at local markets, but suddenly, the markets get canceled due to bad weather. Instead of giving up, you decide to sell your crafts online or at pop-up shops to reach customers.

Ways to be adaptable and flexible:

1. Stay Open-Minded: Be willing to consider new ideas and approaches, even if they're different from your original plan.
2. Be Willing to Change: Don't be afraid to adjust your plans if needed. It's important to be flexible and go with the flow.
3. Stay Positive: Keep a positive attitude, even when things don't go as planned. This will help you stay motivated and find solutions to problems.
4. Learn from Mistakes: See setbacks as opportunities to learn and improve. Use them to make better decisions in the future.
5. Communicate Effectively: Keep your team informed about changes and work together to find solutions. Good communication is key to being adaptable and flexible.

If your plans do not go as expected, how will you address them to stay on track?

_____
_____
_____
_____
_____

WEEK 1

The After Unit:

In the "After Unit," the primary goal is to ensure that outcomes from customer interactions feed back into the initial stages of the business cycle, effectively closing the loop, and initiating a new cycle. This is the phase where businesses strategize on how to capitalize on existing customer relationships to fuel future growth and engagement. Your actions in this phase will help facilitate a seamless transition from post-purchase interactions to potential opportunities for further engagements.

This involves generating customer referrals, creating touchpoints for referral opportunities, upsells, or new projects, and organizing customer appreciation events.

Generating Customer Referrals:

This involves encouraging existing customers to recommend your products or services to others in their network. This can be achieved through various strategies such as referral programs, incentivized promotions, and providing exceptional customer experiences that naturally prompt word-of-mouth recommendations.

A sample simple email of customer referral and review in one:

Subject: Can you please give us a review?

Hi ~Contact FirstName~,
Thank you very much for being a very valued customer of ours and placing the trust in us to provide _____ (Your Services).

~Contact FirstName~, Can you please help us by answering two simple questions?

1. Would you consider us worthy of referring to a friend of yours? Yes No (Yes Link goes to a referral form and No link goes to another form of why they don't think you are worthy of a referring to a friend)

2. Can you please be kind enough to devote a couple of minutes to writing an honest review by clicking on the link below?

(Link to where you want the review to be posted)

Once the page loads please look on the right side of the page and click on write a review. You may need to log into your Gmail account. You will see a screen like this on the right side of the page as it appears below and just click on write a review.

(Install Pictures of the place where they would be posting a Google review)

Would highly appreciate your contribution and an honest review.

Your review is very important to us.

To your Success,

_____

How do you encourage satisfied customers to refer your business to others?

_____
_____
_____
_____
_____

What system do you have for your customers to make them look good and shine in front of their referrals?

_____
_____
_____
_____
_____

Creating Touchpoints for Referral Opportunities and Upsells

This involves strategically designing moments of interaction with existing customers to encourage them to refer others to your business or to consider purchasing additional products or services.

For example, suppose you run a subscription-based meal delivery service. You can create touchpoints by sending personalized emails to existing customers thanking them for their loyalty and offering them exclusive referral discounts or incentives for referring friends or family.

WEEK 1

Additionally, you can include referral prompts or links in your regular newsletters or order confirmation emails, prompting customers to easily share their positive experiences with others.

Similarly, for upsells, you can create touchpoints by displaying relevant product recommendations or upgrades during the checkout process or on the customer account dashboard. You can also send targeted email campaigns highlighting complementary products or services based on the customer's purchase history or browsing behavior.

What touchpoints can you implement to stay engaged with your existing customers?

_____
_____
_____
_____
_____

How can you identify opportunities to upsell additional products or services to your current clients?

_____
_____
_____
_____
_____

Initiating New Projects from Existing Clients

Initiating new projects from existing clients involves identifying opportunities to expand the scope of your services or collaborate on new ventures based on the needs and interests of your current client base.

For example, if you're a graphic design agency and you've been working with a client on branding and marketing materials, you can initiate a new project by proposing to design their website or create social media graphics to enhance their online presence. Alternatively, if you're a software development company and you've developed a custom application for a client, you can suggest additional features or modules to improve the functionality and meet evolving business requirements.

To initiate new projects from existing clients effectively, it's essential to maintain open communication and actively listen to their feedback and challenges. Additionally, demonstrating the value of expanding your partnership through case studies, testimonials, or pilot projects can help build trust and confidence in your ability to deliver results.

Overall, initiating new projects from existing clients requires a proactive approach, creativity, and a deep understanding of their business needs to foster long-term relationships and drive mutual success.

How do you leverage your existing client base to generate new project opportunities?

What strategies do you employ to identify potential new projects or service offerings based on your current client relationships?

Organizing Customer Appreciation Events
Organizing customer appreciation events involves planning and hosting gatherings or activities aimed at expressing gratitude to your clients for their continued support and loyalty. These events serve as opportunities to strengthen relationships, foster goodwill, and show appreciation for their business.

For example, a financial advisory firm might host a client appreciation dinner at a local restaurant, where clients can enjoy a complimentary meal and network with other attendees. A software company might organize a user conference or seminar, featuring product demonstrations, industry speakers, and networking opportunities for clients to connect and share insights.

Week 1

To organize successful customer appreciation events, it's important to consider factors such as the preferences and interests of your clients, the logistics of the event venue and catering, and any special activities or entertainment that will enhance the experience. Additionally, effective communication and promotion of the event, including invitations, reminders, and follow-up communications, are crucial to ensure maximum attendance and participation.

During the event, focus on creating a welcoming and enjoyable atmosphere where clients feel valued and appreciated. Provide opportunities for clients to interact with your team members, share feedback, and provide testimonials or referrals. Offering small tokens of appreciation, such as branded merchandise or personalized gifts, can further enhance the impact of the event and leave a lasting impression on attendees.

Overall, organizing customer appreciation events is an important aspect of relationship-building and customer retention strategies, helping to foster loyalty, strengthen connections, and generate goodwill among your client base.

What types of events or activities would your customers appreciate as a token of gratitude for their loyalty?

How do you think you can personalize these events to make your customers feel valued and appreciated?

Great job on addressing these questions and implementing corresponding actions in the "After Unit!" Let's look into Reflecting and Refining your project.

After: Reflecting and Refining: After finishing a project, it's important to think about what happened and make things better. This means looking

BECOMING A
PIONEER

at everything you did, from the beginning to the end, and figuring out what went well and what didn't. You learn from both the things that worked and the things that didn't and use that to do better next time. It's like when sports teams watch videos of their games to see what they did right and what they can do better for the next game. We will reflect on the experience and identify areas for improvement.

Reflection on the Experience: Thinking back on the whole project is important for getting better and growing. Stepping back helps you see things clearly and look at what went right and what could have gone better. You'll look at the good things and the not-so-good things to learn from them and do better next time. It's like looking at the highs and lows of the project to see what worked and what could have been done differently.

What were the primary successes of the project?

_____
_____
_____
_____
_____

What factors contributed to your achievement?

_____
_____
_____
_____
_____

What are the key lessons learned from this project experience?

_____
_____
_____
_____
_____

Week 1

How do you plan to apply them to future projects to drive continuous improvement?

_____

_____

_____

_____

_____

Identification of Areas for Improvement: As you think about your project, it's important to find areas where you can make things better. This means finding specific parts of the project that could be done better or improved.

What were the standout successes of the project?

_____

_____

_____

_____

_____

Where do you see opportunities for improvement?

_____

_____

_____

_____

_____

Can you find any parts of the project that could be improved or made better to get better results next time?

_____

_____

_____

_____

_____

How will you deal with both the things that went well and the things that didn't, so you can figure out what needs to change to make the project better next time?

_____

_____

_____

_____

_____

As we moved from planning to doing, we saw our ideas turning into action, like following a clear path toward our goals. Every step of making things happen was carefully guided to keep progress fast and purposeful. By using resources well and managing risks carefully, we faced challenges with strength and determination, keeping going even when things were unsure.

Now, as we think back on our journey, we see how important it was to be able to change and adapt when things kept changing. We're happy about the things we did well and we're okay with the things that didn't work out because they help us learn and get better. As we go forward, let's keep making our plans better, using what we've learned to keep getting better and better.

WEEK 1

Kudos on completing the above task. You have just succeeded in creating a framework for mastering the art of systemizing your task.

In Week 1, we embarked on a journey of mastering the art of systematizing everything, beginning with the foundational phases of Before, During, and After. We explored the critical importance of laying the groundwork before diving into any undertaking, akin to gathering ingredients before baking a cake. Through strategic planning and meticulous preparation, we set the stage for success, ensuring that our objectives were clearly defined and our approach was carefully strategized.

Before you head off to week two, please be sure to check out the next page where you will have the chance to build the dominos from this chapter for structuring your sustainable systems for you and your team. This will make it easy for you and your team to be the "sustainable and recurring systems leader."

P.S.: Attached on the next pages are also valuable resources that will be of immense help to you.

Week 1

Your Chapter Dominoes

Build Your Before-During-After System Below:

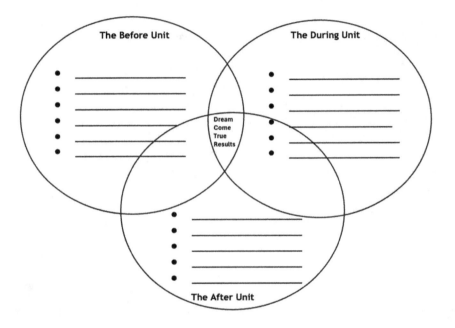

WEEK 1

Useful Resources

QR Code to scan and get all FREE Tools and Resources:

Link from the QR Code:

https://linktr.ee/TheOneYearBreakthrough

Link to all my events:

https://www.eventbrite.com/o/bimal-shah-7943115300

BECOMING A
PIONEER

Time to Celebrate

Before you move to the next chapter, take time to celebrate.

Here are five little ways you can celebrate:

1. Have a foot spa.
2. Buy a new gadget.
3. Watch a live stage performance.
4. Attend a concert.
5. Take a nap in the hammock.

Week 2

Inside the Toolbox: Processes, Checklists, and Beyond

I used to wonder how everything flows in a business, thinking that there must be a process for building a process. So, I started asking myself a lot of questions. Now, I know that when you turn everything into a process, you make it so much better. Let me share a story.

There was a 21-year-old advertising company that was facing serious financial problems. Even though they'd been around for a while, they were struggling to stay afloat. The big issue? They were banking on landing huge $500,000 contracts from each customer. But it was risky. Sometimes they'd hit the jackpot, but other times they'd come up empty, leaving their funds running dry.

They wanted me to help. After looking closely at how they operated, I saw they needed a major change to survive. Instead of waiting endlessly for those big contracts, I suggested they aim for smaller wins. I set up a plan where they could make $25,000 in just two weeks by providing a guaranteed ROI to the customer. It was a big win for the customer and a big shift from their old way of doing things, which could drag on for seven months with no guarantee of success.

This new approach made a huge difference. They started landing customers with every presentation they made, turning their fortunes around. Plus, they now had an 80% chance or more of snagging those $500,000 contracts they'd been dreaming of. It was a game-changer for their business.

In business, it's important to see everything as a step-by-step process. That means every task, like talking to customers or making products, should have a clear plan. Starting with the end goal in mind helps us understand what we want to achieve. It's like knowing where we want to go before, we start the journey. When we know the end goal, we can work better and make smarter choices along the way. This also helps us see any problems that might come up and figure out how to solve them. So, starting with the end goal in mind helps us stay focused and reach our goals more easily.

What do you believe would be the biggest benefits of starting with the end in mind?

_____
_____
_____
_____
_____

Now, I will guide you through the process of building your business operations, along with a series of mindset exercises, thinking tools, actions, and next steps on how to turn everything into a process.

Identify Frontstage and Backstage

In your business operations, there are two crucial stages: Frontstage and Backstage. This two-stage process was originally coined by Erving Goffman[1]. Let's break down these concepts:

Frontstage Processes: Frontstage processes are those directly involved in customer-facing activities. These are the processes that customers interact with, shaping their experience with your business. Examples include sales, customer service, product delivery, scheduling appointments, and online browsing and checkout processes. These processes are visible to customers and play a significant role in shaping their perception of your brand.

Identify the stages of frontstage processes within your business that directly impact customer experience.

1._____
2._____
3._____
4._____
5._____

Backstage Processes: On the other hand, backstage processes are the internal operations that support frontstage activities. These are the behind-the-scenes processes that enable your business to function smoothly. Examples include inventory management, supply chain logistics, and administrative tasks. While not directly visible to customers, backstage processes are essential for ensuring efficiency and effectiveness in delivering frontstage services.

What are the different backstage processes in your business operations?

1._____
_____
2._____
_____
3._____
_____
4._____
_____
5._____
_____

Ways to Improve Frontstage Processes:

Improving frontstage processes involves more than just the visible interactions customers have with your business. It requires a clear understanding and alignment of two crucial elements: commitments from your team and takeaways by your customers.

Commitments from your team entail setting explicit expectations and responsibilities for each team member regarding their roles in customer-facing activities.

For instance, in a retail environment, this could mean ensuring prompt and courteous customer assistance, maintaining comprehensive product knowledge, and actively engaging with customers to fulfill their needs. These commitments establish consistency and professionalism, vital for positive customer experiences.

Equally important are the takeaways by your customers, which represent the tangible benefits or outcomes they derive from engaging with your frontstage processes. For instance, in a restaurant setting, takeaways could include receiving delicious and well-presented meals promptly, along with attentive and friendly service. These positive takeaways directly influence customer satisfaction and loyalty, driving repeat business and positive word-of-mouth referrals.

These two elements can create a structured and efficient framework that enhances the overall customer experience and strengthens your business reputation.

Here are more ways to improve front-stage processes in your business[5]:

1. Training employees: Ensure that staff members are well-trained in customer service skills and product knowledge to provide excellent service to customers.

2. Streamlining processes: Simplify front-stage processes to minimize wait times and ensure a smooth and efficient customer journey.

3. Implementing technology: Use technology solutions such as customer relationship management (CRM) systems or self-service kiosks to enhance customer interactions and improve efficiency.

4. Gathering feedback: Regularly solicit feedback from customers to identify areas for improvement and make necessary adjustments to front-stage processes.

Ways to Improve Backstage Process:

Improving backstage processes involves more than just internal operations; it requires attention to key elements that ensure smooth functioning and contribute to overall business success. One crucial aspect is the delivery of better-than-expected results, which involves consistently exceeding internal performance standards to provide exceptional value to customers. For example, in a manufacturing setting, this could mean

Week 2

implementing quality control measures that result in products surpassing industry standards, thus delighting customers with superior performance or durability.

Additionally, soliciting feedback for improvement at each stage from the customer is essential for refining backstage processes. This feedback loop allows businesses to gather valuable insights directly from customers, enabling them to identify areas for enhancement and address any pain points effectively. For instance, in a software development company, regular user testing and feedback sessions can help uncover usability issues or bugs, leading to iterative improvements that align with customer needs and preferences.

Furthermore, creating opportunities for building credibility, such as through customer reviews and testimonials, enhances the reputation of backstage processes. Positive reviews from satisfied customers serve as powerful endorsements, fostering trust and confidence in the organization's products or services.

Here are more ways to improve backstage processes:
1. Automating tasks: Use automation tools and software to streamline back-stage processes such as inventory management or administrative tasks, reducing manual effort and potential errors.
2. Improving communication: Enhance communication channels between different departments or teams involved in back-stage operations to ensure smooth coordination and collaboration.
3. Investing in training and development: Provide training and development opportunities for employees involved in back-stage processes to enhance their skills and knowledge, leading to improved performance and efficiency.
4. Conducting regular reviews: Regularly review back-stage processes to identify bottlenecks or areas for improvement, and implement changes as needed to optimize performance and effectiveness.

BECOMING A
PIONEER

What are the different commitments you have for your customers at each of your frontstage processes?

1._____
_____
2._____
_____
3._____
_____
4._____
_____
5._____
_____

What are the different takeaways you have for your customers at each of your frontstage processes?

1._____
_____
2._____
_____
3._____
_____
4._____
_____
5._____
_____

What are the top ten steps can you take to improve the efficiency and effectiveness of both frontstage and backstage processes to enhance overall business performance?

1._____
_____
2._____
_____
3._____
_____
4._____
_____
5._____
_____
6._____
_____

WEEK 2

7._____

_____

8._____

_____

9._____

_____

10._____

_____

What would be a recent experience where frontstage or backstage processes played a significant role in shaping customer perceptions of your brand?

_____

_____

_____

_____

_____

Based on the above experience, what changes or improvements, if any, do you need to make to your frontstage and backstage processes?

_____

_____

_____

_____

_____

Good job on completing the task above. Building effective frontstage processes is crucial for delivering exceptional customer experiences. Let's proceed to how to build frontstage processes and teams. On the next page, I am providing a tool to help you visually identify the processes, the team, and their interconnection.

The tool will also help you imagine the step-by-step approach we will build after you have jotted down all the processes and the team representing them.

Processes for "The Dream Come True Experience" for The Customer				
No.	Front Stage Processes	Team	Back Stage Processes	Team

Step-by-Step Approach

Start by carefully examining every way your customers interact with your business. Think about each step they take, from when they first reach out to you to when they need help after making a purchase. Identify the most important moments and actions they take during their journey, such as contacting your sales team or receiving product delivery.

Once you understand these interactions, break them down into smaller, manageable steps. For example, if they're inquiring about your products, consider the process they go through to get the information they need.

Then, create plans for each step to ensure everything goes smoothly for your customers. Determine who is responsible for each task, set deadlines, and establish clear communication channels to keep everyone informed.

When you carefully organize your customer interactions in this way, you can ensure that every interaction they have with your business is efficient and satisfying.

Have you mapped out each stage of your customer interactions, including key touchpoints and activities from initial contact to post-purchase support? ❏ Y   ❏ N

Are you able to identify the sequence of actions required at each stage to ensure a smooth and seamless experience for your customers? ❏ Y   ❏ N

Have you created workflows that outline the steps involved in customer interactions, breaking them down into manageable tasks? ❏ Y   ❏ N

Great job! Now that you understand workflows and customer interaction, let's investigate how to leverage examples and templates to create checklists, workflows, and SOPs.

Different types of SOPs and how and when to use them:

To make customer interactions smoother, use examples and templates for checklists, workflows, and standard operating procedures (SOPs). These different guidelines will help your team follow set procedures, reducing mistakes and working more efficiently.

Text Checklists:
When the SOP is a Text Checklist:
❏ When you must make sure all the elements of a specific job are done to do it right
❏ When you must make sure all the proper tools and things are taken with you to the job site to do the job
right
❏ When you must check everything before take-off (like airplanes- technicians have a checklist when they check everything on an airplane)
❏ When you are performing technical aspects of your job (software or hardware or any other technical job) you must make sure each element is done properly.
Please see the sample checklists provided to understand how to write an effective checklist.

55 NE 5th Avenue, Suite 402
Boca Raton, FL 33432
www.TheOneYearBreakthrough.com

How to Prepare a Good Checklist?

Core Essentials for a Good Checklist:

- ☐ Company Name, logo, and relevant information in the header to make it an official document
- ☐ Title of the checklist- indicating what the checklist is about
- ☐ Instructions on putting a ✓ in each ☐ given at the top of the checklist
- ☐ Each point is posed as a question – Example Did you …..? Human mind responds better to a question than a statement
- ☐ In the end there should be blank lines to provide an explanation for any of the ☐ that are not ✓
- ☐ It should have the signature and date of the person (position) responsible for filling out the checklist. Example:

         _____   _____
         Name of Technician   Date

         _____
         Signature of Technician

TM & © Rajparth 2014-2020 Rajparth Achievers, LLC. This integral concept may not be reproduced in any way shape or form without the written permission of the Publisher, Rajparth Achievers, LLC. Made in Florida, USA.

Week 2

55 NE 5th Avenue, Suite 402
Boca Raton, FL 33432
www.TheOneYearBreakthrough.com

Sample Checklist

Sales/Approval :

Please put a ✓ in each box completed and sign and date this form.

- ☐ Did you Upload in Builder Trend as a Lead Opportunity?
- ☐ Did you Attach the following:
    - ☐ Contract Uploaded?
    - ☐ Intake Form Uploaded?
    - ☐ HOA Affidavit Notarized?
    - ☐ City Affidavit Needs Wet Signature- No Digital Copies- Uploaded?
    - ☐ Did you Upload the completed Commission Sheet?
- ☐ Do the Commission Sheet, Intake Form and The Finance Portal Match?
- ☐ Did you Schedule an Activity in Lead Opportunity for Finance Approval?

If unable to ✓ any of the boxes above, please provide reasons or circumstances below:

_____
_____
_____
_____

_____
Name of the Sales Professional

_____   _____
Signature of the Sales Team Member   Date

TM & © Rajparth 2014-2020 Rajparth Achievers, LLC. This integral concept may not be reproduced in any way shape or form without the written permission of the Publisher, Rajparth Achievers, LLC. Made in Florida, USA.

Visual Instruction:

When the SOP is a VISUAL Instruction:

❏ When you must provide a picture of specific elements to refer to. For example – referring to certain items on the screen like "click on this icon that looks like this."

❏ When you must show specific visual designs or elements in your process to help navigate to the next steps.

Flowcharts:

When the SOP is a Flowchart:

❏ When you are faced with several "IFTTT" (If This Then That) in the process, you need flowcharts as the process may lead to different directions when preparing the process.

❏ There are different connecting elements, and each element has a different possibility and direction to be taken but they all could lead to the same result.

Training Videos:

When the SOP is a Training Video:

❏ When you must provide specific training on how to do a specific process or procedure and it requires either showing specific hardware material or elements on the screen to get it done right and easily, training videos are very useful.

❏ Every training video must accompany a quiz that anyone watching it must take to demonstrate a complete understanding of the training.

❏ The quiz can be done in Microsoft Teams or Google Forms, and you can assign a score for each question and require to one retake the quiz as many times as necessary until they get it right.

Recorded Workshops:

When the S.O.P. is a Recorded Workshop:

❏ When you must provide hands-on training to team members in the field or a group workshop, a recorded workshop is a good idea. For example, there may be specific hardware or specific physical elements that need to be shown and taught that can only be done hands-on or in a group workshop-type setting so others can see how it needs to be done.

❏ Every recorded workshop must come with a quiz or a test to demonstrate a complete understanding of the workshop.

Week 2

Here's a brief step-by-step guide on how to use these guidelines and templates[3]:

1. Identify Needs: Determine the specific areas where your team could benefit from checklists, workflows, or standard procedures.

2. Find Examples: Search for examples of checklists, workflows, and standard procedures relevant to your industry or business needs.

3. Adapt Templates: Modify these examples to fit your specific requirements, such as adding or removing steps, clarifying instructions, or customizing formats.

4. Share with Team: Distribute the adapted templates to your team members, ensuring they understand how to use them effectively.

5. Train Team: Provide training or guidance on how to follow the checklists, workflows, and standard procedures correctly.

6. Monitor and Update: Regularly review and update the templates as needed based on feedback, changes in processes, or new best practices.

Customize the templates to fit your business and customer needs. In short, using templates makes customer interactions easier and ensures consistency and quality in your services.

Based on the guidelines above, what are the different checklists, training videos, workshops, flowcharts, visual instructions, and documented processes you need to create?

_____
_____
_____
_____
_____
_____
_____
_____
_____
_____

Assembling the Team: Now that you have the list of SOPs, assemble a dedicated team to delegate the outcome of preparing all the SOPs. This team should consist of individuals with strong communication skills, a customer-centric mindset, and a commitment to delivering exceptional service.

Good job! Let's proceed to how you can develop efficient Back Stage Processes.

Build Backstage Processes and Team

Developing efficient backstage processes is crucial for the smooth operation of internal functions. Start by identifying key areas of internal tasks and workflows that require streamlining and optimization. Once these areas are identified, use the guidelines provided earlier for best practices such as creating checklists, procedures, and workflows. Clear documentation is essential as it helps in improving operational efficiency by providing a framework for consistency and clarity.

How do you currently approach the development of backstage processes within your organization?

Can you identify specific areas of internal operations that could benefit from improved processes?

How do you plan to document and communicate these backstage processes to ensure clarity and consistency among your team members?

Week 2

What metrics or indicators will you use to measure the effectiveness of your Back Stage processes?

_____

_____

_____

_____

_____

How will you track progress toward optimization of your backstage?

_____

_____

_____

_____

_____

Creating Checklists, Procedures, and Training Materials:

Creating checklists, procedures, and training materials is essential to support backstage processes effectively. These resources serve as a roadmap for team members, ensuring consistency and clarity in their roles and responsibilities.

Do your checklists and procedures address challenges in your business?
❑ Y ❑ N

If yes, then that's great. If not, go back and make sure those checklists and procedures address the challenges as much as you can to the best of your ability.

Forming an Efficient Back Stage Team

Assembling an efficient backstage team is vital for the successful management and execution of internal processes. Begin by identifying key roles and responsibilities required to support backstage operations, ensuring that each team member has a clear understanding of their tasks.

The key roles required to support backstage operations may vary depending on the specific needs of the organization. However, some common key roles may include:

1. Operations Manager: Responsible for overseeing all backstage operations, including planning, organizing, and coordinating activities to ensure smooth workflow and efficient resource allocation.

BECOMING A
PIONEER

2. Inventory Manager: Manages inventory levels, ordering, and stock control to ensure sufficient supplies are available while minimizing excess inventory and associated costs.

3. Logistics Coordinator: Coordinates the transportation and distribution of goods, ensuring timely delivery and efficient routing to minimize shipping costs and maximize customer satisfaction.

4. Procurement Officer: Responsible for sourcing and purchasing goods and services required for backstage operations, negotiating contracts with suppliers, and ensuring cost-effective procurement practices.

5. Administrative Assistant: Provides administrative support to backstage operations, including managing documentation, scheduling appointments, and coordinating meetings to facilitate smooth workflow and communication within the team.

6. Quality Control Inspector: Conducts quality checks on incoming materials and finished products to ensure compliance with quality standards and specifications, identifying and resolving any issues or discrepancies.

These are just a few examples of key roles that may be necessary to support backstage operations. The specific roles and responsibilities will depend on the nature of the business and its operational requirements.

Select individuals with the necessary skills and expertise to fulfill these roles effectively, considering factors such as experience, qualifications, and compatibility with the team dynamic. To foster collaboration and communication, implement strategies such as regular team meetings, clear communication channels, and shared documentation platforms. Encourage open dialogue and feedback to facilitate smooth coordination and workflow management, ultimately driving efficiency and productivity within the Back Stage team.

What criteria do you need to build when selecting team members to manage backstage processes?

_____
_____
_____
_____
_____

WEEK 2

What steps do you need to take to ensure that each member is aligned with the organization's goals and values?

_____

_____

_____

_____

_____

Do you have an outcome-based job description outlined for each of your team members? ❏ Y   ❏ N

If yes, then that is great. If not, please access the sample outcome-based job description below to prepare one for each of your team members.

https://bit.ly/TheIdealJobDescription

You need to build accountability measures and ownership of results and outcomes for each team member.

What measures and standards will you build to instill accountability and ownership in your team members?

_____

_____

_____

_____

_____

Beginning with a fundamental understanding of distinguishing between frontstage and backstage operations, the chapter emphasizes the significance of each in delivering seamless customer experiences and ensuring internal operational excellence. You have been guided through a step-by-step process of identifying frontstage processes related to customer-facing activities and backstage processes focused on internal operations.

Once the frontstage and backstage processes are identified, you can build these processes and assemble the teams necessary for execution. I also provided practical advice on creating checklists, workflows, and standard operating procedures (SOPs) for customer interactions, enabling businesses to standardize practices and ensure consistency in service delivery. Additionally, I shared insights on assembling teams with

BECOMING A
PIONEER

the requisite skills and expertise to manage both frontstage and backstage operations effectively.

Furthermore, you cannot overlook the importance of adaptability and continuous improvement in process development and team management.

Congratulations on completing this chapter! You have learned how to create processes for everything, ensuring that your business stays successful. In the next chapter, I will teach you how to systemize all your platforms. This will ensure that your employees understand all the technology that is available to leverage and use daily.

Before you head off to week three, please check out the next page, where you will have the chance to write dominos from this chapter to focus on the superpower you need every day to build a solid frontstage and backstage company so that you can deliver great profitability consistently.

P.S.: Attached on the next pages are also valuable resources that will be of immense help to you.

Week 2: Domino Effect

Your Chapter Dominoes

Build Your Frontstage and Backstage Structure Below:

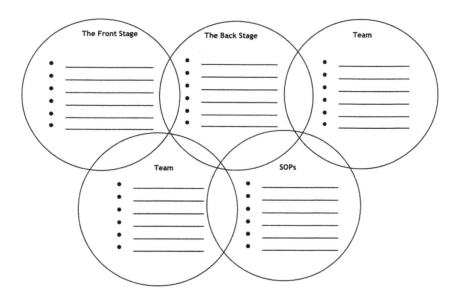

Useful Resources

QR Code to scan and get all FREE Tools and Resources:

Link from the QR Code:

https://linktr.ee/TheOneYearBreakthrough

Link to all my events:

https://www.eventbrite.com/o/bimal-shah-7943115300

Week 2

Time to Celebrate

Before you move to the next chapter, take time to celebrate.

Here are five little ways you can celebrate:

1. Visit a nearby museum.
2. Declutter your wardrobe.
3. Attend a baseball/basketball/football game.
4. Invent your own groovy dance steps.
5. Explore Spotify playlists.

Week 3

All Your Platforms to Systematize

I used to think that you could use Google platforms that are Free, and you should be able to do everything. When my business started scaling, I realized that you cannot completely rely on the free platforms, and you will run into limitations. Many paid platforms have good technological and business capabilities that can make it very easy for you.

Technology platforms play a pivotal role in streamlining operations and maximizing efficiency in today's world of business. Businesses rely on these platforms to automate tasks, organize data, and facilitate communication within organizations.

Here are more than a dozen project and task management software:

Software Name	Features	Pros	Cons	Price Range	Purpose	Ideal Usage
Trello®	Kanban boards - Task assignments - Due dates	User-friendly interface - Flexible customization - Free basic version	Limited reporting capabilities - Not suitable for complex projects	Free - $17.50/ user/month	Task management, Agile workflows	Small to medium-sized teams, simple project tracking

Becoming a
PIONEER

Asana®	Task lists - Assignments - Deadline tracking	Intuitive design - Strong collaboration features - Free version available	Steeper learning curve for advanced features - Limited customization	Free - $24.99/ user/month	Task and project management	Teams of all sizes, especially those focused on task-oriented projects
Monday. com®	Customizable boards - Timeline views – Automation	Visual and intuitive interface - Versatile project tracking - Robust integrations	Can become expensive for larger teams - Steeper learning curve for complex setups	$8 - $24/ user/month	Project management, team collaboration	Teams of all sizes, especially those with complex workflows
Base-camp®	To-do lists - Message boards - File sharing	Simplified interface - Centralized communication - All-in-one platform	Limited task management features - Lacks advanced project tracking	$99/month (flat rate)	Team collaboration, project communication	Small to medium-sized teams, simple project management
Wrike®	Gantt charts - Task dependencies - Time tracking	Powerful reporting tools - Advanced project planning features - Scalable for large teams	Complex interface for beginners - Pricing may be prohibitive for some	$9.80 - $24.80/ user/month	Project planning, resource management	Medium to large-sized teams, complex project requirements
ClickUp®	Task lists - Time tracking - Customizable dashboard	Highly customizable - Robust feature set - Affordable pricing plans	Overwhelming for some users due to extensive features - Steeper learning curve	Free - $9/ user/month	Task management, project planning	Teams of all sizes, particularly those looking for flexibility and customization
Smart-sheet®	Spreadsheet-style interface - Collaboration tools – Automation	Familiar interface for Excel users - Advanced reporting capabilities - Highly customizable	May feel too basic for advanced project management needs - Not as intuitive for non-Excel users	$14 - $25/ user/month	Project tracking, resource management	Medium to large-sized teams, data-driven projects
Team-work®	Task lists - Milestone tracking - Time tracking	Strong task management features - Intuitive interface - Good integration options	Limited customization options - Pricing may be high for some users	$10 - $18/ user/month	Project planning, team collaboration	Small to medium-sized teams, task-oriented projects

WEEK 3

Jira®	Issue tracking - Agile boards - Custom workflows	Powerful for Agile teams - Extensive customiza-tion options - Strong integration ecosystem	Steep learn-ing curve for beginners - Overkill for simple projects	$7 - $14/ user/month	Agile project management, software de-velopment	Agile teams, software de-velopment projects
Zoho Projects®	Task lists - Gantt charts – Timesheets	Affordable pricing plans - Compre-hensive project plan-ning tools - Integration with other Zoho apps	Interface can be cluttered - Limited automation capabilities	$3 - $6/ user/month	Project plan-ning, team collaboration	Small to me-dium-sized teams, sim-ple project tracking
Microsoft Teams®	Collaboration platform for online meetings and business communication. Offers video conferencing, file sharing, and real-time collaboration.	Excellent for team collabo-ration, offers top-notch cybersecurity standards, and inte-grates with Microsoft 365	Not a project management software	Subscrip-tion Starts at $4 per user per month	Improve team commu-nication and collaboration	It is ideal for Teams that want to com-municate ef-ficiently and effectively
Slack®	Real-time mes-saging, channels, huddles, work-flow automation	Free Plan available, 2500 plus integrations, automated workflows on all paid plans, mul-tiple built-in communica-tion options, very easy-to-use.	Expensive plans, mes-sage history gets buried, limited users in huddles.	Free to $7.25 per user per month.	Communi-cation and collaboration app.	For business of all sizes.
Google Work-space®	Business email service, Google Drive, Docs, Sheets, Slides, Calendar, Meet	Access to great digital products, seamless integration with tools designed to aid collabo-ration, docu-ment sharing, scheduling, and more.	Learning curve due to wide array of features and integrations.	Starts at $6 per user per month	Facilitate enterprise creation, productivity, and mobility	For businesses that need a centralized place for brain-storming, discussion, ad collabo-ration.

Microsoft 365®	Includes Word, Excel, PowerPoint, and depending on plan, other services like Outlook.	Constant updates and support for its productivity software, cloud storage, and deep collaborative features.	Subscription-based, so requires a monthly fee.	Starts at $12.50 per user per month.	Productivity and collaboration	For small businesses and large enterprises.
Dropbox®	Best-in-class sync technology, 256-bit AES and SSL/TLS encryption, industry-leading security, and privacy.	User-friendly interface, rich feature set, great value for money.	Limited email templates, complexity of advanced features, strict compliance rules.	Starts at $11.99 per month for a Premium Plus account offering 2TB of storage4.	Data storage and sharing	For users who want more than the 2GB of storage

Now let's look at each platform focusing on the purpose, best use, and investment range:

1. Trello: Trello is a versatile project management tool designed for organizing tasks and workflows using Kanban boards. It is best used for agile project management, task tracking, and team collaboration. Trello offers a free basic version with limited features, while the paid plans range from $0 to $17.50 per user per month, catering to both individuals and businesses of all sizes.

2. Asana: Asana is a popular task and project management platform known for its intuitive interface and robust collaboration features. It is best used for organizing tasks, managing projects, and fostering team communication. Asana offers a free version with basic features, and its paid plans range from $0 to $24.99 per user per month, making it suitable for teams of all sizes.

3. Monday.com: Monday.com is a flexible work operating system that allows teams to plan, track, and manage projects in various formats, such as boards, timelines, and calendars. It is best used for project management, team collaboration, and workflow automation. Monday.com offers pricing plans ranging from $8 to $24 per user per month, making it accessible to teams with different budgetary requirements.

4. Basecamp: Basecamp is an all-in-one project management and team collaboration platform designed to simplify communication and task management. It is best used for organizing projects, sharing files, and facilitating team discussions. Basecamp offers a flat-rate pricing model of $99 per month, providing unlimited users and projects, making it ideal for small to medium-sized teams.

5. Wrike: Wrike is a powerful project management software equipped with advanced planning and collaboration features, including Gantt charts, task dependencies, and real-time collaboration. It is best used for project planning, resource management, and team collaboration. Wrike offers pricing plans ranging from $9.80 to $24.80 per user per month, catering to medium to large-sized teams with complex project requirements.

6. ClickUp: ClickUp is a customizable productivity platform that offers a wide range of features for task management, project planning, and team collaboration. It is best used for organizing tasks, creating workflows, and managing projects across different teams and departments. ClickUp offers a free version with limited features and paid plans ranging from $0 to $9 per user per month, making it suitable for teams of all sizes and budgets.

7. Smartsheet: Smartsheet is a collaborative work management platform that combines the familiarity of a spreadsheet with powerful project management capabilities. It is best used for project tracking, resource management, and data-driven projects. Smartsheet offers pricing plans ranging from $14 to $25 per user per month, providing a scalable solution for medium to large-sized teams.

8. Teamwork: Teamwork is a comprehensive project management software designed to streamline task management, milestone tracking, and team collaboration. It is best used for project planning, task delegation, and team communication. Teamwork offers pricing plans ranging from $10 to $18 per user per month, catering to small to medium-sized teams with varying project needs.

9. Jira: Jira is a popular software development tool known for its robust issue tracking, agile project management, and customizable workflows.[6] It is best used for software development projects, Agile methodologies, and team collaboration. Jira offers pricing plans ranging from $7 to $14 per user per month, making it suitable for Agile teams and software development projects.

10. Zoho Projects: Zoho Projects is a cloud-based project management platform equipped with tools for task management, Gantt charts, and timesheets. It is best used for project planning, team collaboration, and task tracking. Zoho Projects offers pricing plans ranging from $3 to $6 per user per month, providing an affordable solution for small to medium-sized teams.

11. Microsoft Teams: Microsoft Teams is a cloud-based collaborative platform for online meetings and other business communication needs. It offers top-notch cybersecurity standards and multi-factor authentication to keep teams connected and organized. Though it was only introduced in 2017, it's become a go-to tool for project teams of all sizes. Microsoft Team Essentials starts at $4 per user per month and the Microsoft 365 Business Standard runs at $12.50 per user per month.

12. Slack: Slack is a cloud-based collaboration software that helps teams streamline their communications and improve their productivity. It prioritizes real-time communication and integration capabilities, so its users can enjoy a platform that enables them to centralize their teams' communications and integrate seamlessly with other tools. Slack offers a free tier with limited features, alongside three premium tiers, namely the Pro, Business+, and Enterprise Grid plans. It goes from Free to $7.25 per user per month.

13. Google Workspace: Google Workspace (formerly known as G Suite) is Google's comprehensive suite of cloud-based productivity and collaboration tools, which includes Google's business email service. This professional email service is one of the core offerings of Google Workspace, enabling businesses to use custom, branded email addresses that match their domain name.

Apart from Gmail, Google Workspace includes several other tools like Google Drive, Docs, Sheets, Slides, Calendar, Meet, and many more. These tools are all integrated to provide a seamless work environment where teams can collaborate effectively, in real-time, from any part of the world. Google Workspace plans start with the Business Starter. At a palatable $6/user/month, it gets you a business email, video meetings for 100 folks, and 30GB of cloud storage per user - along with solid security. For those needing more, the Business Standard, at $12/user/month, adds meeting recording, bumps up participants to 150, and shoots your cloud storage to a mighty 2TB/user. If you're in the big leagues, the

WEEK 3

Business Plus plan at $18/user/month amps up meetings to 250 participants, hands you 5TB cloud storage per user, and gifts you advanced security and management controls.

14. Microsoft 365: Microsoft 365 works on all your computers and mobile devices and includes collaborative features and perks. Microsoft launched its 365 service in 2011 to help modernize the Office suite. The subscription model allows Microsoft to offer constant updates and support for its productivity software, along with cloud storage and deep collaborative features.

Microsoft 365's individual plan costs $7 a month. So, if you were to buy the standard $150 Office suite, you would need to use it for 21 and a half months for it to be more cost-effective than Microsoft 365. Individuals who buy the $250 Office Home and Business bundle for Outlook access need to use the software for about 35 and a half months before they start "saving" money. (If you're a business buying Microsoft software for multiple computers, then you would need to stick with Office for even longer before you start "saving" money, as 365 Business starts at just $5 per person per month.)

15. Dropbox: Dropbox offers features that will appeal to both personal and business users. Dropbox has continued to evolve since its launch in 2008, adding new features and always aiming to outdo the competition. Dropbox offers impressive performance throughout all its features. Dropbox has some of the best-integrated tools on the market. Privacy and security are disappointing, to say the least. The service should appeal to those looking for collaboration within teams.

Opening an account with Dropbox gives you 2GB of free storage space. With the free account, you can sync your files across three devices and restore older files for up to 30 days. Dropbox keeps its paid plans simple. Personal users can choose either the Plus or Family plan, which offers the same 2TB of storage space. Both plans for personal use allow you to rewind files for up to 30 days and transfer files up to 2GB in size.

The main difference is that the Plus plan is intended for a single user, while the Family plan allows up to six people on the same plan. On the Dropbox Plus plan, 2TB of storage costs $11.99 per month. Comparatively, iCloud and Sync.com offer better value. You can enjoy 2TB of storage for around $8 per month.

BECOMING A
PIONEER

Do you currently leverage any technology platforms in streamlining your business? ❑ Y ❑ N

No doubt, the adoption of technology platforms has enabled businesses to optimize their workflows and allocate resources more effectively from digitizing manual tasks to centralizing information. It has become easier for organizations to streamline their operations, reduce errors, and minimize time-consuming manual efforts.

What are some specific manual tasks within your organization that you believe could be automated or digitized to improve efficiency?

_____
_____
_____
_____
_____

However, selecting the right technology platforms is crucial for businesses looking to systematize their processes effectively. It's essential to assess the specific needs and objectives of the organization and choose platforms that align with these requirements. Whether it's enhancing customer interactions, managing projects more efficiently, or improving internal communication, each technology platform should serve a distinct purpose and contribute to the overall success of the business.

What criteria do you consider when selecting new systems or tools?

_____
_____
_____
_____
_____

It is safe to say that technology platforms serve as indispensable tools for modern businesses seeking to streamline their operations and drive growth. The power of technology has made it possible for organizations to optimize their processes, improve efficiency, and gain a competitive edge in the market.

WEEK 3

How do you see technology platforms benefiting your business by optimizing processes, improving efficiency, and giving you a competitive edge in the market?

_____

_____

_____

_____

_____

Good job! You are doing well. Now let's proceed to types of technological platforms to systemize your business process.

We have various technology platforms for systematizing business processes. Several categories stand out for their widespread use and effectiveness. These include project management platforms, CRM (Customer Relationship Management) systems, ERP (Enterprise Resource Planning) solutions, and collaboration tools. Each category serves a specific purpose and offers unique features tailored to different aspects of business operations.

Are you familiar with these various types of technology platforms?
❑ Y ❑ N

Which ones do you currently use or plan to implement in your organization?

_____

_____

_____

_____

Project management platforms are designed to help teams plan, organize, and execute projects efficiently. They typically offer features such as task management, milestone tracking, and team collaboration tools. CRM systems, on the other hand, focus on managing customer interactions and relationships. They centralize customer data, track communication history, and facilitate sales and marketing activities.

Do you envision leveraging project management and CRM platforms for your business? ❑ Y ❑ N

ERP solutions integrate various business functions and processes into a single system, streamlining operations and promoting data consistency across departments[2]. They often include modules for finance, inventory management, human resources, and more. Collaboration tools, such as messaging apps and document-sharing platforms, foster communication, and collaboration among team members, regardless of their physical location.

How do you see ERP systems and collaboration tools contributing to the efficiency and effectiveness of your organization's overall operations?

_____
_____
_____
_____
_____

As technologies help businesses, however, understanding the functionalities and benefits of different types of technology platforms is essential for optimizing business processes and enhancing productivity. It is how you leverage these platforms strategically that can help your organization streamline operations, improve customer relationships, and drive growth.

Let's reflect on this.

If you were to choose any technological platform, which one would it be?

_____
_____
_____
_____
_____

How do you plan to incorporate it into your business strategy?

_____
_____
_____
_____
_____

Week 3

What challenges do you anticipate in the implementation process?

_____
_____
_____
_____
_____

Now take a 15-second break to stretch. We are about to go deeper. We will delve into selecting technology platforms for your business. The evaluation criteria and how each factor aligns with your business's specific needs and goals.

Selecting Technology Platforms for Your Business

When picking technology platforms for your business, it's important to have a clear way to decide which one is best for you. Start by thinking about factors like scalability. This means how well the platform can grow and change as your business does. Other things to think about include usability, cost, and whether the platform meets your specific needs.

I am providing a tool on the next page that I have created to help you select the right technological platform and software for your business.

BECOMING A
PIONEER

The Technology Evaluator™

Deciding on The Right Technology for Your Business

RAJPARTH ACHIEVERS

Name: _____
Cell: _____ Email: _____
Start Date: _____ End: _____

What is the End Result you will achieve with this technology?					
What is the Total Investment over a Three year Period (X)			Learning and Set Up Time		
YES	Start Date: _____				
What top one to five current time consuming activities will it eliminate?	Time Eliminated (A)	$ Value - (C)	What are the Top one to three replacement activities will it create?	Time Taken (B)	$ Value of Time (D)
Total Time Saved (A-B) If not +ve, It is a NO.			Total Value Savings (If C-D not 5 X- It is a No)		

TM & © Rajparth 2014-2020 Rajparth Achievers, LLC. This integral concept may not be reproduced in any way shape or form without the written permission of the Publisher, Rajparth Achievers, LLC. Made in Florida, USA.

WEEK 3

The Technology Evaluator™

Deciding on The Right Technology for Your Business

Name: _____
Cell: _____ Email: _____
Start Date: _____ End: _____

| What current problem will it solve? | |
| Total Cost of Problem to the Business over three years | |

Start Date for the Best Alternate: _____

NO			
What other alternate activities or strategies would solve the same problem without the use of Technology?	Time Taken (E)	$ Value of Time (F)	Check ✓ if you want to pursue this alternate or strategy
Total Time Saved (E-C)		Total Value Savings (F -C)	

TM & © Rajparth 2014-2020 Rajparth Achievers, LLC. This integral concept may not be reproduced in any way shape or form without the written permission of the Publisher, Rajparth Achievers, LLC. Made in Florida, USA.

BECOMING A
PIONEER

What factors do you consider when choosing technology platforms for your business?

_____
_____
_____
_____
_____

What was the reason why you didn't pick a platform you wanted for your business?

_____
_____
_____
_____
_____

Integration capabilities are another critical aspect to evaluate, as seamless integration with existing systems and tools can enhance efficiency and data consistency across your organization.

How do you plan to integrate new technology platforms with your current infrastructure?

_____
_____
_____
_____

User-friendliness is another important key. It is essential for widespread adoption and effective utilization of technology platforms among your team members. Evaluate the platform's interface and usability to ensure that it aligns with the skill levels and preferences of your workforce[7].

How would you rate the user-friendliness of your current technology platforms?

_____
_____

Cost-effectiveness is a key consideration, encompassing not only the initial investment but also ongoing maintenance and support costs. Conduct a thorough cost analysis to understand the total cost of ownership and the return on investment offered by each platform.

What is the total cost of ownership for your current technology platforms?

_____

_____

Given a large budget, what platform would you opt for immediately?

_____

_____

_____

_____

_____

Lastly, prioritize platforms that offer robust customer support and ongoing updates to address issues and incorporate new features. Evaluate the vendor's reputation, responsiveness, and availability of support resources to ensure a positive long-term partnership.

How would you rate the quality of customer support provided by technology platform vendors? ❑Average ❑Below Average ❑Good ❑Very Good ❑Excellent

Now you can see that developing a comprehensive evaluation criteria framework based on scalability, integration capabilities, user-friendliness, cost-effectiveness, and customer support is essential for selecting technology platforms that align with your business needs and goals.

So, ask yourself: Are you satisfied with your current technological platform? ❑ Y ❑ N

Let's reflect on the case studies of businesses that leveraged technology platforms to systemize their process. We will extract key lessons and apply them to your own business.

Here are two examples of businesses that have effectively leveraged technology platforms:

1. Salesforce:

Salesforce, a leading provider of CRM (Customer Relationship Management) software, offers a comprehensive platform that allows businesses to streamline their sales, marketing, and customer service processes[4]. Salesforce centralizes customer data, automates repetitive tasks, and provides actionable insights. It helps businesses enhance their customer engagement and drive revenue growth. Salesforce has made it easier for businesses to systematize their sales and marketing processes, track customer interactions, and manage leads effectively.

2. Amazon:
Amazon, the multinational technology company, has revolutionized the retail industry with its advanced logistics and fulfillment platform. Through its sophisticated network of warehouses, distribution centers, and transportation services, Amazon has optimized its supply chain operations to deliver products to customers with unprecedented speed and efficiency. The company leverages technology platforms to systemize its processes for inventory management, order fulfillment, and delivery logistics, meeting the growing demands of online shoppers worldwide.

3. Asana:
Asana leverages its project management software to streamline internal workflows, manage tasks efficiently, and improve team collaboration. They centralize project-related information and provide a platform for real-time communication. Asana helps teams stay organized, prioritize tasks, and achieve project goals effectively.

4. Trello:
Trello harnesses its intuitive task management platform to facilitate project planning, task tracking, and team collaboration. Through its visual boards and customizable workflows, Trello empowers teams to organize tasks, track progress, and collaborate seamlessly, thereby enhancing productivity and project transparency.

5. Monday:
Monday.com maximizes its work operating system to optimize project management, task tracking, and team coordination. With its customizable features and flexible interface, Monday.com enables teams to create tailored workflows, automate routine tasks, and streamline project execution, ultimately driving efficiency and productivity.

6. Microsoft Teams:
Microsoft Teams utilizes its collaboration platform to facilitate seamless communication, virtual meetings, and document sharing among team members. It integrates chat, video conferencing, and file collaboration features. Microsoft Teams enables remote teams to stay connected, col-

laborate effectively, and achieve project milestones irrespective of their location.

7. Slack:
Slack leverages its real-time messaging platform to foster communication, collaboration, and knowledge sharing within organizations. The platform replaces email with instant messaging channels, accelerates communication, reduces email overload, and promotes a culture of transparency and teamwork across teams and departments.

8. Keap:
Keap leverages its CRM and marketing automation software to streamline customer relationship management, automate marketing campaigns, and drive sales growth. With its lead nurturing capabilities, personalized marketing automation, and sales pipeline management features, Keap empowers businesses to engage leads, convert prospects, and retain customers effectively.

9. Constant Contact:
Constant Contact harnesses its email marketing platform to create engaging email campaigns, nurture customer relationships, and drive business growth. Through its user-friendly interface, customizable templates, and robust analytics, Constant Contact enables businesses to design, send, and track email campaigns that resonate with their audience and achieve marketing objectives.

10. Basecamp:
Basecamp utilizes its project management software to facilitate collaboration, task management, and project tracking for teams. With its straightforward interface and essential project management features, Basecamp simplifies project coordination, enhances team communication, and ensures accountability, leading to improved project outcomes.

11. Mailchimp:
Mailchimp leverages its email marketing platform to automate email campaigns, segment audiences, and analyze campaign performance. Mailchimp provides tools for email design, audience segmentation, and campaign optimization. Mailchimp also empowers businesses to create targeted email campaigns, drive engagement, and achieve marketing goals effectively.

These examples illustrate how businesses across different industries have successfully utilized technology platforms to systematize their processes and achieve operational excellence.

From these case studies, we can see the challenges faced by businesses during the implementation of technology platforms, ranging from resistance to change among employees to compatibility issues with existing systems. You can also anticipate potential obstacles and develop strategies to overcome them proactively.

What are some common challenges that you have encountered when implementing new technology platforms?

_____
_____
_____
_____
_____

How did you address them?

_____
_____
_____
_____

What solutions and strategies have you employed to address future challenges?

_____
_____
_____
_____

In conclusion, it is important to pick the right platforms that fit your business goals. I suggest checking out the platforms we've mentioned more, trying them out, and asking others for advice before deciding.

Going forward, readers need to do some careful research. They should look into how well a technology platform can grow with their business, how easily it can work with other systems, and how easy it is for people to use. They should also make sure that any plan they come up with for putting the technology in place matches up with what their organization wants to achieve.

Week 3

Great job on completing Week 3! You've learned how to select the best technology platforms to streamline your business processes. We've stressed the importance of choosing platforms that match your business needs and goals. In Week 4, get ready to dive into 'The Five Dials Dashboard'. I'll introduce a thorough framework for keeping track of and improving important performance metrics in your business operations. Before moving on to Week 4, be sure to check out the helpful resources provided on the next page.

Before you head off to week four, please check out the next page, where you will have the chance to write dominos from this chapter to focus on building your customized secret formula that makes you a great daily results leader that you can use every day for the rest of your life.

P.S.: Attached on the next pages are also valuable resources that will be of immense help to you.

Week 3

Your Chapter Dominoes

Reflecting on various technology platforms we learned in week 3.

1. Which platforms have you chosen for each specific purpose outlined in the chapter?

2. What budget have you allocated for each of the selected platforms?

3. How do these choices align with your business goals and budget constraints?

WEEK 3

Useful Resources

QR Code to scan and get all FREE Tools and Resources:

Link from the QR Code:

https://linktr.ee/TheOneYearBreakthrough

Link to all my events:

https://www.eventbrite.com/o/bimal-shah-7943115300

Time to Celebrate

Before you move to the next chapter, take time to celebrate.

Here are five little ways you can celebrate:

1. Watch your favorite movie on Netflix.
2. Do some scrapbooking.
3. Repaint your room/house.
4. Practice your handwriting and calligraphy.
5. Start a bonfire at a camp and make smores.

Week 4

The Five Dials of The Rinse and Repeat Systems

When I was initially building systems and processes, I used to think that every system needs to be different and have different elements. Now I know that the systems that you build need to be replicable. They need to be recurring in nature and you need to be able to have rinse and repeat systems.

Rinse and repeat means you have repeatable, monotonous systems in business that deliver predictable results. After building several systems and processes for businesses, I have realized that there are five core dials that you need to focus on when you build these replicable systems.

In business, it's important to know how well your company is doing so you can make smart choices and help it grow. Imagine your business is like a car, and just like a car has important gauges to tell you how it's doing, your business has five important measures too. These dials are the important dials that you always pay attention to when running a business just like you pay attention to when driving your car. You can only pay attention when they are on a dashboard and that's why cars and planes have dashboards. Your business needs one too.

When you drive you keep an eye on the following five dials:

1. Speed: This is to see how fast you are going and not driving at an unsafe speed.
2. RPM: You look at your RPM (revolutions per minute) to prevent engine strain and maintain fuel efficiency.
3. Fuel: To see how far you can go before you have to refuel.
4. Temperature: Overheating can damage the engine so maintaining the right temperature always is essential.
5. Oil Gauge or Light: Low oil pressure can harm the engine, so the indicator is essential.

A pilot also keeps an eye on specific five gauges while flying: Attitude, Air Speed, Altimeter, Vertical Speed, and Heading Indicator.

All humans and animals have five fingers on their hands. There is a big significance of the five elements. Business owners should focus on five key dials for their systems in businesses. Initially, I thought I had to juggle every aspect of my business, feeling overwhelmed. But then, I realized that like a car's dials, there are five essential dials for every rinse-and-repeat system you build in business.

The five dials for every system you build in business are as follows:

1. **Specificity:** Every system needs a clearly defined purpose and outcome. The more specific you are about the system, the better it will turn out to be.
2. **Benchmarks:** A system without benchmarks is destined to fail. You need to have very clear benchmarks at every stage in the system to gauge the effectiveness of the system.
3. **Accountability:** A system cannot succeed without accountability of the people and the processes. You need to have an accountability structure built at every benchmark and result.
4. **Timing:** The "time-in" and the "timing" are both critical when building replicable systems and processes. Clear timelines must be established for each benchmark, each result, and each outcome to be achieved by each team member.
5. **Quantification:** Nothing is complete without measurable results. The systems you built need to have numbers that you can look at that can tell you if you are doing things in business bigger, easier, faster, or cheaper. "Better" is not a measurable term and it is a perception- so you must define better in measurable terms.

Week 4

Now that you have a basic idea of the five dials you need for systems in your business, it is time to build specifics for each of those and understand the five dials you want to have.

On the next pages, I am providing you a tool to guide you on building a solid foundation on how to keep track of the five dials and have it on your business dashboard when building systems and processes. These five dials and the structure in each will provide you a blueprint to build effective rinse-and-repeat systems in your business that significantly improve your bottom line. You must keep in mind that when you build everything that makes a positive and meaningful transformation for your ideal customer, you cannot go wrong with your systems.

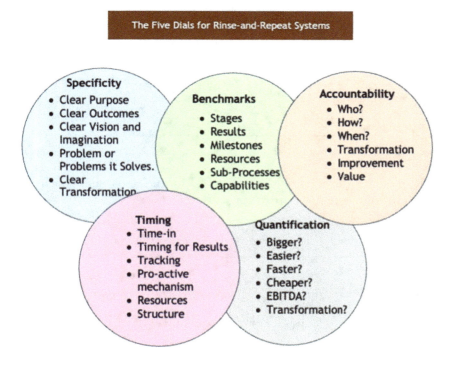

BECOMING A
PIONEER

What are the 5 dials for the systems you want to build in your business?

1._____

2._____

3._____

4._____

5._____

How will you bring "Specificity" to each of your systems and processes in your business?

_____

_____

_____

_____

_____

What will be your method to create "Benchmarks" for each of your systems and processes?

_____

_____

_____

_____

_____

Who and how will you hold "Accountable" for the results and benchmarks in your systems or processes?

_____

_____

_____

_____

_____

How will you arrive at the "Timing" and "Time in" for each of the results in the system?

_____

_____

_____

_____

_____

Week 4

How will you "Quantify" the overall efficiency of the systems and processes you built?

_____

_____

_____

_____

_____

One of my clients, a building company, wanted to ensure that vehicle assets were tracked and that there was visibility of what was in the truck when it went from point A to point B. It turns out that there is already software available for this purpose. Similarly, there are many examples of platforms that I have illustrated in the chapter.

To keep a close eye on the success, it's crucial to identify five key elements that act as indicators. These dials give insights into different parts of your business, such as sales, customer satisfaction, and efficiency. By understanding these elements, you get a clear picture of what keeps your business moving and where you can make improvements.

What are some examples of key elements that could serve as dials for monitoring your business's well-being?

_____

_____

_____

_____

_____

How do you determine which metrics or indicators are most relevant to your specific business goals and objectives?

_____

_____

_____

_____

_____

Can you explain how regularly tracking these key dials has contributed to better decision-making and strategic planning for your business?

_____

_____

_____

_____

_____

Great job. This will lead us to examples and suggestions for common metrics.

Examples and Suggestions for Common Metrics:

Most of the time, you don't have to reinvent the wheel; it's already there. Numerous platforms can be used for various purposes in a business, and I will share them with you below.

When selecting the five key dials for your business's dashboard, it's essential to choose metrics or indicators that accurately reflect the critical aspects of your operations. Here are 5 key elements and let's elaborate on each of the five key dials with appropriate examples:

1. Retained Earnings: This refers to the portion of the net operating income of the business that is retained within the company for reinvestment. For instance, if a business earns $100,000 in net operating income and decides to retain $30,000 for reinvestment, the retained earnings would be $30,000. This can be illustrated by tracking the balance of the Growth account in the three-bucket cash flow system, where funds are earmarked for future business growth initiatives.

2. Profitability per Employee: Payroll is typically a significant expense for companies, and it's crucial to ensure that the gross contribution margin is substantial enough to cover employee payroll costs. For example, if a company has a gross contribution margin of $200,000 and incurs $40,000 in employee payroll expenses, the profitability per employee would be $200,000 divided by the number of employees. Ideally, this ratio should be at least five times the employee payroll to ensure healthy profitability and sustainability.

3. Improvement Percentage of Customer Values: This metric involves tracking the improvement of customer values over time, including Individual Transaction Value (ITV), Average Customer Value (ACV),

Week 4

and Lifetime Customer Value (LCV) for different customer segments. For instance, if a business observes a 10% increase in ITV and a 15% increase in LCV over 900 days, it indicates positive growth and enhanced customer relationships.

4. Your Uniqueness: This dial pertains to identifying and maintaining the unique selling propositions (USPs) or pioneering aspects of your business that set it apart from competitors. For example, if a company is the only provider of a particular innovative product or service in the market, it demonstrates uniqueness. Tracking customer feedback, market trends, and competitor analysis can help maintain and enhance this uniqueness over time.

5. Sales Improvement Ratio: This metric measures the improvement in sales performance on both a monthly and annual basis. For instance, if a business achieves a 20% increase in monthly sales compared to the previous month and a 15% increase in annual sales compared to the previous year, it reflects positive sales growth. Monitoring sales data regularly allows businesses to identify trends, adjust strategies, and capitalize on opportunities for continuous improvement.

Which of these key elements align most closely with your business objectives and strategic priorities?

_____
_____
_____
_____
_____

Are there any additional metrics specific to your industry or niche that should be included in your Five Dials Dashboard?

_____
_____
_____
_____
_____

How do you plan to collect and track data for each of these metrics to ensure accuracy and reliability?

_____

_____

_____

_____

_____

What tools or software platforms can you leverage to automate data collection and reporting for your Five Dials Dashboard?

_____

_____

_____

_____

_____

Here's a guide to help you build your 5 dials and the measurements they need to monitor along with steps to improve them[10]:

1. Identify Key Metrics: Begin by identifying the most critical metrics that drive your business's success. These could include financial metrics like revenue growth, profitability, and cash flow, as well as operational metrics like customer satisfaction, employee productivity, and sales effectiveness.

2. Set Targets: Once you've identified the key metrics, set specific targets or goals for each one. These targets should be realistic yet challenging, providing a clear direction for improvement.

3. Establish Monitoring Systems: Implement systems to monitor and track each metric regularly. This could involve using software tools, spreadsheets, or dashboards to collect and analyze data in real time.

4. Analyze Performance: Regularly analyze the performance of each metric against your targets. Identify any areas where performance is below expectations and investigate the root causes.

5. Take Action: Based on your analysis, take proactive steps to address any issues or inefficiencies identified. This could involve implementing process improvements, training programs, or strategic initiatives to drive performance improvement.

WEEK 4

6. Review and Adjust: Continuously review the effectiveness of your actions and adjust your strategies as needed. Be flexible and willing to adapt to changing circumstances to ensure ongoing improvement.

As you embark on the process of identifying the Five Dials for your business dashboard, it's crucial to align your choices with your specific business goals and priorities. Here's why:

1. Relevance: Your business goals serve as the guiding force behind your operations. Select metrics that directly relate to these goals to ensure that your dashboard provides meaningful insights into progress and performance.

2. Focus: With countless metrics available for tracking, it's easy to become overwhelmed. Focusing on your business goals helps you narrow down the selection to those metrics that truly matter and have the most significant impact on your success.

3. Alignment: When your Five Dials align with your business goals, every decision and action taken to improve those metrics contributes directly to achieving your overarching objectives.

4. Flexibility: As your business evolves and priorities shift, so too may your chosen metrics. You must regularly reassess and realign your Five Dials with your current goals so that your dashboard remains relevant and actionable.

Building the Five Dials Dashboard:

Creating your Five Dials Dashboard is an essential step in gaining valuable insights into your business's performance. Here's how to get started:

1. Define Your Metrics: Begin by selecting the five key metrics or indicators that will serve as your dials. These should align closely with your business goals and provide actionable insights into critical aspects of your operations, such as sales performance, customer satisfaction, productivity, etc.

What are the five key metrics or indicators that you believe are most critical to monitor for your business's success?

_____

_____

_____

_____

_____

2. Design the Dashboard: Choose a format for your dashboard that allows for a clear and concise display of your selected metrics. Whether using a digital dashboard tool or a physical display board, organize the layout in a way that makes it easy to track progress and identify trends immediately.

How will you organize and lay out your dashboard to ensure that these metrics are displayed in a clear and easily digestible format?

_____

_____

_____

_____

_____

3. Select Tools and Software: Depending on your preferences and technical capabilities, you can choose from a variety of tools and software options for building your dashboard. This could range from simple spreadsheet programs like Microsoft Excel to more advanced dashboarding platforms like Tableau or Google Data Studio.

Have you researched and evaluated different dashboarding tools and software options to determine the best fit for your needs and budget?
❏ Y ❏ N

4. Customize and Configure: Once you've selected your tools, take the time to customize and configure your dashboard to meet your specific needs. This may involve creating custom charts or graphs, setting up automated data feeds, or integrating with other systems and databases to pull in real-time information.

What steps will you take to ensure that your dashboard remains up-to-date and reflective of real-time data?

_____
_____
_____
_____
_____

5. Test and Iterate: Before finalizing your dashboard, be sure to test it thoroughly to ensure accuracy and usability. Solicit feedback from key stakeholders and make any necessary adjustments or refinements based on their input. Remember, your dashboard should evolve to reflect changes in your business priorities and goals.

How will you communicate and share your dashboard with relevant stakeholders to stay up-to-date?

_____
_____
_____
_____
_____

Scoring and Tracking Mechanisms:
Establishing scoring and tracking mechanisms for each of the Five Dials is crucial for effectively monitoring your business's performance and progress toward goals. Here's how to implement these mechanisms:

1. Define Metrics: Start by clearly defining the specific metrics or KPIs (Key Performance Indicators) that align with each of your Five Dials. These metrics should be quantifiable, relevant to your business objectives, and actionable.[8]
What specific metrics or KPIs will you track for each of your Five Dials?

_____
_____
_____
_____
_____

Why are these metrics important to your business?

Set Benchmarks or Targets: Once you've identified your metrics, establish benchmarks or targets to measure performance against. This could involve setting specific numerical goals, such as revenue targets, customer satisfaction scores, or productivity levels, to strive for.

How will you determine benchmarks or targets for each metric?

What factors will you consider when setting these goals?

Track Progress: Implement a system for tracking progress against your established benchmarks or targets. This may involve regularly collecting and analyzing data, updating your dashboard with real-time information, and monitoring trends over time.

What methods or tools will you use to track progress against your benchmarks?

How frequently will you review and update your data?

_____

_____

_____

_____

_____

Visualize Data: Utilize visualizations or charts to represent your data in a clear and understandable format. Bar graphs, line charts, and pie charts are commonly used to visualize performance metrics and trends, making it easier to identify areas of improvement or success.

In what ways will you visualize your data to make it more understandable and actionable for yourself and your team?

_____

_____

_____

_____

_____

5. Adjust and Iterate: Continuously monitor and evaluate your performance metrics, and be prepared to adjust your targets or strategies as needed. Use your tracking mechanisms to identify areas where performance is falling short and take proactive steps to address any issues or challenges.

How will you use the insights gained from your tracking mechanisms to inform strategic decisions and drive continuous improvement in your business operations?

_____

_____

_____

_____

_____

Monitoring and Adjusting:
Regularly monitoring the Five Dials Dashboard is essential for staying informed about your business's performance and making informed decisions. Here are effective ways to manage this process:

BECOMING A
PIONEER

1. Regular Monitoring: Schedule regular check-ins to review the data on your Five Dials Dashboard. This could be daily, weekly, or monthly, depending on how often the data updates and the nature of your business operations. Consistent monitoring will keep you informed about any changes or trends affecting your business.

How frequently do you monitor your Five Dials Dashboard?

_____
_____
_____
_____
_____

2. Interpreting Data: Take the time to interpret the data displayed on your dashboard. Look for patterns, trends, or anomalies that may indicate areas of strength or areas needing improvement.

What are the things you look for when monitoring your dashboard?

_____
_____
_____
_____
_____

3. Identifying Areas for Improvement: Use the insights gained from your dashboard to identify areas of improvement or concern within your business.

Are there any dials that consistently fall below target? ❑ Y ❑ N

Are there areas needing improvements from insights gained from your dashboard? ❑ Y ❑ N

Identifying these areas allows you to proactively address issues and drive positive change.

4. Taking Action: Once you've identified areas for improvement, take appropriate actions to address them. This could involve implementing new strategies, reallocating resources, or revising existing processes.

WEEK 4

How do you plan to address the areas of concern or opportunity identified through your dashboard analysis?

_____

_____

_____

_____

_____

5. Remaining Agile: Finally, recognize that business conditions can change rapidly, requiring you to adapt your approach accordingly. Stay agile and flexible, adjusting your Five Dials and tracking mechanisms as needed to align with evolving business goals and circumstances. Regularly reassess your dashboard metrics and update them as necessary to ensure they continue to provide meaningful insights into your business's performance.

How will you ensure that your Five Dials and tracking mechanisms remain relevant and aligned with your evolving business goals and priorities?

_____

_____

_____

_____

_____

In conclusion, the Five Dials Dashboard serves as a powerful tool for business owners and executives to monitor and manage key aspects of their operations effectively. Throughout this chapter, we explored the importance of identifying the five key elements critical to monitoring the pulse of the business and discussed strategies for building, scoring, and tracking the dashboard.

As you embark on implementing your own Five Dials Dashboard, it's essential to tailor the metrics and tracking mechanisms to align with your specific business goals and priorities. Regular monitoring and interpretation of the dashboard insights will enable you to stay agile and adaptive, adjusting strategies and tactics as needed to navigate changing market conditions and achieve long-term success.

Remember, the Five Dials Dashboard is not just a static tool but a dynamic framework that evolves with your business. As you move forward,

BECOMING A
PIONEER

I encourage you to embrace the Five Dials Dashboard for your business management strategy, empowering you to take your business to the next level and help you achieve your goals.

High five for coming to the end of this chapter, which marks the end of this book. You have successfully learned how to systematize everything in your business. I can't wait to hear about your success story.

In the next book, I will walk you through how to install accountability for you and your team. Results are what matters, and the next book will show how you install, track, and get accountability at each step flawlessly on autopilot.

But, before you head off to Book # 10, please check out the next page, where you will have the chance to get the dominos from this chapter that can assist you in never forgetting what "Systemize Everything" is all about.

P.S.: Check out the free resources provided for your continued success on the next pages.

Week 4

Your Chapter Dominoes

Build Your Foundational Five-Dials System below:

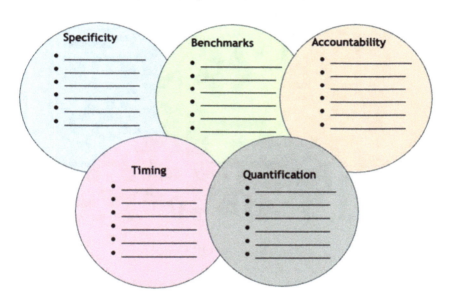

Useful Resources

QR Code to scan and get all FREE Tools and Resources:

Link from the QR Code:

https://linktr.ee/TheOneYearBreakthrough

Link to all my events:

https://www.eventbrite.com/o/bimal-shah-7943115300

Week 4

Time to Celebrate BIG!!

Before you move to the next chapter, take time to celebrate BIG as you have learned a foundational system for "Systemizing all your processes" for improvement beyond your imagination.

Here are five ways you can celebrate:

1. Have the best massage of your life.
2. Grill barbecues.
3. Camp out in a tent next to your home.
4. Practice with your guitar or other musical instruments.
5. Catch up on your sleep.

BECOMING A
PIONEER

Hidden Insights from this Book
Doubling Your Business and Taking Over Your Industry in a Year!

Below, I have provided proven uncharted bottom-line insights from this book to double your business and rise in your industry in a year:

1. The Before-During-After System
There is a Before-During-After for every aspect of your business and every function. Think of the B-D-A in everything you do and every activity. Make it part of your life, and your business, and you will see so much clarity and transformation.

2. Inside The Toolbox: Processes, Checklists and Beyond
Whenever something unforeseen happens in your business, go back and ask yourself a question- Could this have been prevented from happening with a better process, checklist, instruction, training, SOP, Flowchart, or Workshop?

3. The Platform Paradox: Solving Business Challenges with Technology
You don't have to maximize the use of every platform to get your money's worth. All you have to do is use the elements that get you 5 times or more of what you pay for the platform.

4. The Five Dials For Rinse-and-Repeat Systems.
Just like when you close all your fingers to make a fist that has power, only when the five dials are working together, do you have absolute power and efficiency.

DON'T FORGET

Join The Pioneers Club for FREE!

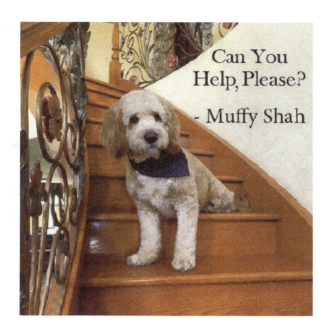

Thank You for Reading My Book!

I appreciate your reading this book!

I would love it if you can give me an honest review.

I need your input to make the next version and my future books better.

Please leave me a helpful 5-star review on Amazon, letting me know. what do you think?

Thank you so much!
—Bimal Shah

BECOMING A
PIONEER

Please don't forget to check out the next book—on becoming the most effective "results leader" for your team and your customers.

This is the next step in the sequence of steps to Becoming a Pioneer by achieving your three-year goal in one year.

See you in book 9!

DON'T FORGET

Join The Pioneers Club for FREE!

With the purchase of each book, you are Eligible to Join the Club Meeting for FREE

Connect with Pioneers around the World—Every Month. With the book purchase, you are a member. No strings attached.

Connect with Me and walk away with personalized insights for you in the Club meetings held every month on
Wednesdays at 6 PM EST.

Walk away with a customized 30-Day Action Plan at each meeting.

Get Your FREE Membership at: https://bit.ly/ThePioneersClub.

Conclusion

My dear friend and fellow entrepreneur we have come to the end of book 9. It's been an awesome journey. This book if used appropriately will help you become a daily results leader in just 4 weeks.

The book asks deep questions that call for self-reflection. Please take your time to go through the questions, and perform the exercises given. Because they will help you greatly in systematizing everything.

I believe that I have given you everything I can to help you become the ideal leader and take your business to the next level, thereby helping you achieve your full entrepreneurial potential, and be the entrepreneur God called you to be.

Bye for now. See you in book Ten.

About the Author

Bimal Shah is an accomplished Senior Executive, Entrepreneur, Advisor, Coach, and Results Leader with more than twenty years of success in the financial services industry. Leveraging extensive experience in growth, entrepreneurship, talent development, financial reporting systems, profitability systems, and processes to scale, he is an asset for companies spanning various industries, sizes, and stages of growth that are seeking expert assistance in bringing their business to the next level. His broad areas of expertise include executive coaching, strategic planning, operations management, scaling, and growth.

As a breakthrough coach, Bimal has successfully helped companies generate growth of more than 50 percent in a year and has taken 52 companies to exponential growth in a year. Through his unique hiring process technique, he has helped dozens of companies hire highly qualified C-level employees. He has worked with more than fifty companies, providing coaching and financial consulting services across an array of industries, including manufacturing, distribution, home health care, communications, security systems, and professional services. His unique Coaching-Planning-Accountability system has generated favorable results in record time for CEOs, reducing their working hours, in six months, by 35 percent.

As a result, CEOs see exponential company growth within a year, can hire smart and productive team members at all levels within a few months, and receive the tools to develop effective "out of the box" marketing strategies.

Bimal is also the founder of Rajparth Advisory Group (2005), which provides financial consulting services to entrepreneurs. From 1996 to 2005, before founding Rajparth Group, he worked as an independent advisor through Northwestern and New York Life, helping more than 1000 families preserve their assets, reduce their taxes, increase their income, and create everlasting legacies.

During his tenure, he was awarded the highest honor in the industry, The Million Dollar Round Table—Top of the Table Award for six years in a row, and the Global Corporate Award for Best Life Insurance Agent in the Asian Indian Community.

Bimal has also authored and published *The Daily Happiness Multiplier*, available on Amazon and in bookstores throughout North America. His unique "Success Deck" consists of 52 Workshop Videos and Tools to positively impact anyone's personal and professional life with a single tool each week for 52 weeks. Bimal earned his Bachelor of Commerce in Economics from the University of Mumbai and his Bachelor of Science in Advertising from the University of Florida. He holds a Chartered Financial Consultant, Chartered Life Underwriter, and Certified Advisor in Senior Living from the American College at Bryn Mar, Pennsylvania.

Some Accolades for Bimal's Work

"Bimal is the big picture guy, and he takes us deep. I might concentrate on one idea that I think is the greatest idea in this world, and Bimal will come back with making us think 10 times bigger and he's got this amazing ability to see opportunity. He lays out a great plan to get to where you want to go and makes it just so attainable. Every entrepreneur with big goals should consider hiring Bimal and if I could have Bimal in my pocket and carry him around always that would be great."

—*Mike Barnhill, Managing Partner, Specialist ID*

"Before, I was working 70–80 hours a week. Now it is down to 45–55 hours a week. The personal impact of his coaching has allowed me to spend more time with my family. The financial impact has been priceless because of the time saved. If you are struggling, consider hiring Bimal. His books and coaching have helped me plan and organize where I want the business to go. Bimal has also taught me to push my limits and think about things more in detail on why I am doing this."

—*Reginald Andre, CEO, Ark Solvers, Inc.*

"Bimal's books and workshops have further reinforced and enhanced some aspects of my leadership; in that, he has brought on a fresh perspective on my role as a leader of the company. In addition to Bimal being a very engaging and energetic personality, he also has an open-minded and unique perspective to making learning a fun-filled experience for my staff, which then adds immeasurable value to my company."

—Terry Sgamatto, Managing Regional Director, Seeman Holtz

"I recently took a leap of faith . . . one that required a consistent amount of convincing myself out of a scarcity mindset and making an investment. It has just been a few weeks and I am very happy with the results of my decision. Under the advisement of Bimal, I have had to make some drastic decisions in my company but have to say overall, even though some were painful, they have all been results-driven and not emotional. I truly appreciate all that Bimal has helped me create in the first few weeks and cannot wait to see what comes next."

—Sarah Martin, CEO, Experience Epic, LLC

"We hired Bimal to get our company better organized and have better business practices and we have been practicing that every year for so many years now. Bimal is a pretty persistent guy, and he doesn't let us get away with being lazy. He pushed us to accomplish the goals we had set to accomplish—you helped us get it done and he didn't let us be lazy at all. If you want to build a self-managing company, Bimal is the guy-- it's worth the effort and time and it's worth the energy that you are going to put into it as you are going to get every bit and more out of it and the amount of money you spent is insignificant compared to the results you have attained."

---Shawn Crow, CEO, Austen Enterprises, Inc.

Notes

Microsoft Teams®: A registered trademark of Microsoft Corporation.
Slack®: A registered trademark of Slack Technologies Limited.
Salesforce®: A registered trademark of Salesforce.com, Inc.
Trello®: A registered trademark of Atlassian.
Monday®: A registered trademark of Monday.com Ltd.
Basecamp®: A registered trademark of Basecamp, LLC.
Wrike®: A registered trademark of Wrike, Inc.
Clickup®: A registered trademark of ClickUp, Inc.
Smartsheets®: A registered trademark of Smartsheet Inc.
Teamwork®: A registered trademark of Teamwork.com Ltd.
Jira®: A registered trademark of Atlassian.
Zoho®: A registered trademark of Zoho Corporation.
Google Workspace®: A registered trademark of Google LLC.
Microsoft 365®: A registered trademark of Microsoft Corporation.
Dropbox®: A registered trademark of Dropbox, Inc.
Amazon®: A registered trademark of Amazon.com, Inc.
Keap®: A registered trademark of Keap, Inc.
Constant Contact®: A registered trademark of Endurance International Group, Inc.
Mailchimp®: A registered trademark of The Rocket Science Group LLC.

1. *Goffman, E. (1959). The Presentation of Self in Everyday Life*

2. *Reinsel, D., Gantz, J., & Rydning, J. (2018). The Digitization of the World from Edge to Core. IDC White Paper, #US44413318. Sponsored by Seagate.*

3. *Gawande, A. (2011). The Checklist Manifesto: How to Get Things Right. Metropolitan Books.*

4. *Salesforce. (n.d.). What is a CRM Platform? Salesforce.com.*

5. *George, M. L., et al. (2004). The Lean Six Sigma Pocket Toolbook: A Quick Reference Guide to Nearly 100 Tools for Improving Process Quality, Speed, and Complexity. McGraw-Hill Education.*

6. *Weill, P., & Woerner, S. L. (2017). Thriving in an Increasingly Digital Ecosystem. MIT Sloan Management Review, 59(1), 13-22.*

7. *Davenport, T. H. (2018). The AI Advantage: How to Put the Artificial Intelligence Revolution to Work. MIT Press.*

8. *Parmenter, D. (2010). Key Performance Indicators (KPI): Developing, Implementing, and Using Winning KPIs. John Wiley & Sons.*

9. *Kaplan, R. S., & Norton, D. P. (1996). The Balanced Scorecard: Translating Strategy into Action. Harvard Business Review Press.*

10. *Harvard Business Review. (2022). How to Design a Dashboard for Your Business. Harvard Business Review.*

Printed in the USA
CPSIA information can be obtained
at www.ICGtesting.com
LVHW011926230524
780938LV00002B/26